I LOVE YOU MORE
THAN YOU KNOW

Also by Jonathan Ames

I Pass Like Night
The Extra Man
What's Not to Love?
My Less Than Secret Life
Wake Up, Sir!

As Editor:

Sexual Metamorphosis: An Anthology of Transsexual Memoirs

I LOVE YOU MORE THAN YOU KNOW

Jonathan Ames

Black Cat

a paperback original imprint of Grove/Atlantic, Inc.

New York

Some of the essays in this book have previously appeared, usually in a somewhat different form, in the following magazines and journals: "The Thick Man," "Oh, Pardon My Hard-On," "Rue St. Denis," "Troubles With Cockroaches and Young Girls," "My Wiener Is Damaged!," "I Called Myself El Cid," "Everybody Dies in Memphis," "No Contact, Asshole!" and "Whores, Writers, and a Pimple: My Trip to Europe" in *New York Press;* "Ron Gospodarski" in *Gear;* "My New Society Testimony: Able to Love Again" in *Bomb;* "Self-Sentenced" and "S/he Said, He Said" in *Bookforum;* "I Love You More Than You Know," "Loose Tiles," and "Snowfall" in www.mrbellersneighborhood.com; "Escape Home," in *The New York Times;* "Club Existential Dread" and "'Tis the Season for Halitosis" in www.mcsweeneys.net; "The Most Phallic Building in the World" and "Midlife Assessment: Cataloging My Ruination" in www.slate.com; "The Most Phallic Building in the World Contest" in www.cabinetmagazine.org; "Kurt Cobain" in www.blacktable.com; "Sneakers Make the Boy" in *Blackbook;* "Jersey Shore" in *Paper;* and *"The Onion* Asks Me: What Is Funny?" in *The Onion.*

The "definitions" in this book first appeared in *The Future Dictionary of America,* published by McSweeney's, and "A Tribute to George Plimpton" first appeared as the introduction to a reissue of Plimpton's novel *The Curious Case of Sidd Finch,* published by Four Walls Eight Windows.

The author and publisher gratefully acknowledge the following for the right to reprint material in the book: P. 62: "Able to Love Again" © Dr. F. A. Mesmer. P. 185: "Williamsburgh Bank Building" © Scott Murphy. P. 186: "Ypsilanti Water Tower" © Mark Heisler. Pp. 216–217: *Out of My League* by George Plimpton. Reprinted by permission of Russell & Volkening as agents for the author. Copyright © 1961 by George Plimpton, renewed in 1989 by George Plimpton. Pp. 219, 227: *On the Road* by Jack Kerouac, © 1955, 1957 by Jack Kerouac, renewed © 1983 by Stella Kerouac, renewed © 1985 by Stella Kerouac and Jan Kerouac. Used by permission of Viking Penguin, a division of Penguin Group (USA) Inc.

FIRST EDITION

Printed in the United States of America
Published simultaneously in Canada

Library of Congress Cataloging-in-Publication Data

Ames, Jonathan.
    I love you more than you know / Jonathan Ames.
        p. cm.

    ISBN 0-8021-7017-X
    I. Title.
PS3551.M42115 2006
813'.54—dc22

2005052748

Black Cat
a paperback original imprint of Grove/Atlantic, Inc.
841 Broadway
New York, NY 10003

06 07 08 09 10   10 9 8 7 6 5 4 3 2 1

For My Great-Aunt Doris

CONTENTS

I LOVE YOU MORE
THAN YOU KNOW

THE THICK MAN

I woke up from a disturbed night's sleep with my sinuses clogged and aggrieved. I had just been dreaming that I had a brain tumor. I hacked and sneezed my way out of bed and cursed my neighbor who smokes cigarettes first thing in the morning. The stink of his tobacco creeps its way into my bedroom each day, awakening me at 8 A.M. and causing an allergic reaction.

So I opened the door of my apartment this particular morning and shouted across the hall, "STOP SMOKING!" and then I slammed my door and muttered, "You bastard." I often do this, but I don't know if he ever hears me. I don't think so since he was friendly to me the other day in the elevator and I feigned civility.

Anyway, after this auspicious beginning an incredible day unfolded. My sinuses drained, and then later that morning a messenger arrived with copies of my new novel, *The Extra*

Man. I usually don't tip messengers, but since this was a special occasion I opened my wallet. I had a twenty, a five, and two singles. I hesitated as to the proper tip amount and then took the two dollars and handed them to the good man. He looked down at the bills and I immediately regretted not giving him the five—what could he do with two dollars? But he thanked me with his French-Haitian accent and an appreciative smile appeared on his face. I forgave myself my cheapness. He can buy a slice of pizza, I thought.

I closed the door and examined my novel. I noticed right away that from the rough handling of the messenger—whom I had just generously endowed with two American dollars—that all three copies had tiny dents in their bindings. They are ruined, I thought. How can I be proud of them?

My insane response to holding my novel for the first time, a novel I had worked on for too many years, fulfilled the prediction of a friend of mine, Spencer, a therapist-in-training. "When you get your book," he had said, "you'll immediately seek out an imperfection and then want to kill yourself." The young Freudian was right. So to prove him wrong, I pretended to ignore the minuscule dents and was able to see that the book was actually quite beautiful, that nine years of waiting for a second novel had come to a fantastic end.

But I couldn't revel in my accomplishment for too long as I had to hustle off and play a role in a short, avant-garde film. A beautiful woman, whom I've had my eye on for six years, had asked me a few days earlier to be in this movie with her. She had initially called to tell me she had seen my one-man show at the Fez and that she admired my performance. I thanked her for her kind words, and then she made her proposition: "Jonathan, I'd like to work with you. I'm shooting this short film Friday with this great director and I think you would be perfect as my lover."

"Your lover? I'm flattered."

"We have to kiss," she said in a whisper.

"It's the role I've been waiting for!" I said, grandly.

"A Hollywood kiss," she then said, disappointing me. "No tongue."

"Of course not," I said, maintaining my dignity.

Still, tongue or no tongue, the opportunity to embrace this woman felt like a gift from heaven; she wanted me to be her lover in a movie—was it to be a warm-up for real life? I could only hope. So after receiving my novel, I rushed off to the movie location. The director had called me the day before and told me to dress like a 1940s businessman—so my costume was my Brooks Brothers sport coat and tie, my Barracuda raincoat, and a fedora I had bought years ago in Saratoga Springs, New York. We were shooting on the plaza in front of the Tisch School at NYU. I arrived on set and my costar greeted me with a compliment. "You look so handsome," she said.

"I think this fedora makes me look like a Hasid," I said.

"Not at all," she said.

"Well, *you* are a picture of beauty," I said, and she was. She's a redhead with high cheekbones, green eyes, and a slender yet womanly figure. She was wearing an old-fashioned-looking black cocktail dress. We were straight out of *The Thin Man*—she was Myrna Loy to my William Powell.

The director was a long-haired fellow with a regal jaw. He positioned us in front of the shiny sculpture which is next to the plaza's Fourth Street entrance. I was to speak no lines. My sole duty was to hold my Myrna Loy and kiss her. The director positioned our arms around one another in a way that he liked.

He explained that Myrna was to kiss my neck, then count to four, swivel her head, and kiss me on the lips. He was going to shoot us while sitting in a wheelchair, pushed around by his assistant. His idea was to circle us for a Hitchcockian embrace, like the one in *Vertigo* with Jimmy Stewart and Kim Novak.

We did the first take. I felt the tender smooch on my neck, then her glorious face swiveled and was before me. Her green eyes flashed, with flecks of gold inside the green. She put her lips on mine and to my great surprise she immediately opened her mouth and this lovely female tongue introduced itself to my male tongue and tickled it hello. We held the kiss. It was delightful, and I swelled against Myrna's thigh, no longer a Thin Man. I grabbed her rear.

"Beautiful, beautiful," the director exhorted, and I sensed him circling us in the wheelchair-cum-dolly for his Hitchcock shot, and there was no hitch to my cock, it rode up her dress looking for a ride home.

"Cut," he said.

Myrna immediately pulled away from me. "How was it?" she asked the director.

"Beautiful. Beautiful. You guys look great."

My erection began to go down. The director reset the shot. The assistant took a light-meter reading. We stood there holding one another. "That was some kiss," I said. "I'm glad it wasn't a Hollywood kiss. It was more French new wave."

"Oh, my God. Did I use my tongue? I was simply in role. I wasn't even aware."

"You didn't feel anything?"

"I was only aware of the camera."

This was dispiriting. Had our kiss meant nothing to her? If she was unaware of her own tongue, was she unaware of my Thick Man?

For the next hour all I did was kiss her. As soon as the director said "Action," I got action. Up my erection would go and then down it would go with the castrating "Cut." And after every embrace, she'd pull away from me and ask the director about the shot. I was falling in love and all she cared about was art. Why had she asked me to do this? What did it all mean?

Then our scene was over. She had many more hours of shooting, but I was done for the day. Done for the film. Myrna gave me a chaste kiss good-bye on the cheek and reapplied her lipstick for her next scene. "Let's talk soon," I said. "Go out for dinner."

"Sure," she said, but there was no indication in her tone that this kissing would have a sequel. I felt resigned. She is a beautiful enigma who gave me an hour of joy and I don't know why; perhaps that is all there will be.

I walked home, sexually wound up and emotionally melancholic, which is a rare combination—depressed and aroused. So I stopped at the Missionary Position Cafe on Second Avenue for a consoling coffee. I sat at one of the tables and a young blonde girl at the adjoining table smiled at me. I am having a curious effect on women these days, I thought.

I brooded over my caffeine. I held my fedora on my lap. The blonde was still looking at me. She was in a blue cotton summer frock. Her arms were delicately covered with gold hairs and she wouldn't stop staring at me.

"Do I know you?" I asked.

"No. But I saw you at the Fez. You are very funny." A conversation ensued. She spoke English well but with a German accent. She was a tourist from Hamburg, nearing the end of a two-week holiday. Her name was Claudia. She was only twenty-one, and she was quite lovely except for a pimple on her right temple. But I forgave her this, thinking that traveling is difficult on one's skin. She had seen my show listed in the *Voice* and had come with several German friends. She thought I was a celebrity. I was in like Flynn. My Fez show was working all kinds of wonders for me. I spent the rest of the day with her. But not wanting to lay out a lot of cash, I took her to Staten Island. You can't beat an inexpensive romantic boat ride. Then I paid for a cheap Italian meal on the Island, and she drank a carafe of wine.

"You don't drink?" she asked.

"No, I'm an alcoholic," I said.

"Doesn't that mean you drink a lot?" she said. They're very smart in Germany.

"I've quit," I said.

"That's good," she said. "My father is an alcoholic. But he drinks." Once she said that, I knew I was in for a good night. The odds had been in my favor ever since she had agreed to go with me to Staten Island, but you never know with women. Sometimes things turn out platonic when you least expect it, especially with European women. In Europe men and women are often friends, which doesn't happen in America, so American men, such as myself, can get confused. We're not accustomed to being friends with females.

But daughters of alcoholics, regardless of their country of birth, often adore me. It's sad, but the lousy fathers of the world have driven all these girls, their heartbroken daughters, into my arms. I'm not sure what these girls see in me—my inherent alcoholism, drunk or sober? the impossibility of lasting love?—but they sniff it out and try to undo what went wrong way back when. Of course they can't. No one can. And what am I looking for? Probably to let somebody down so that I can hate myself.

Anyway, the sun set and we took the ferry back and the sea air made us amorous. We began to kiss on the prow. It was my second French kiss of the day, even though Claudia is German. My fedora almost blew off.

We came ashore and found a secluded bench near the water in Battery Park. I didn't need a director for this scene. Claudia sat on my lap. We kissed. I became aroused and she rubbed herself against my erection.

Then I noticed out of the corner of my eye that the Holocaust Museum was looking right at me. I had forgotten that it was in Battery Park. The museum wasn't happy with my behavior. Forty-five years ago her people were gassing my people. But she's innocent, I thought, protesting to the building. Then Claudia draped herself across my knees and raised her ass. This was unexpected. Then she put my hand against her ass, and I understood intuitively that she wanted me to spank her. She was awfully young to be depraved, but people, generally, are more mature in Europe.

So I lifted her frock, revealing yellow panties. Her ass was round and firm and white. Quite beautiful. I began to lightly spank her rear, though I mixed in a hard smack every now and then to keep her guessing. With my hand cupped, I also tapped her gently between the crack of her buttocks, softly hitting her vulva. She really seemed to like that. Then I looked over at the Holocaust Museum. Is this better? I asked, silently, in my mind. I figured that corporally punishing a German had to give the museum some solace. And while I spanked her, I gave her my thumb to suck as a phallic substitute and she took to it blissfully.

Later, I put Claudia on the subway back to her hotel. She was leaving New York the next day to go to Boston. From Boston, she would fly to Germany. Who knew that Boston had direct flights to Hamburg. We exchanged addresses and kissed good-bye. What will become of her?

I went home and put my copies of *The Extra Man* on my bookshelf. When I was a little boy I used to put my new sneakers next to my bed and stare at them as I went to sleep. I was always proud of new sneakers, thought they were so beautiful-looking. So twenty-odd years later I lay in bed with the light on and stared at the copies of my novel. Across the distance of my room the dents in the bindings were hardly noticeable.

1998

OH, PARDON MY HARD-ON

Saturday night, I was out with my friend the Polish actress and film star Graziela. She's an older woman, wonderfully elegant, and still quite beautiful. She chain-smokes and uses a silver cigarette holder, but with Graziela I don't mind the secondhand smoke. With her, it's like the fog on the stage for an Ibsen play. It's romantic, moody, and provides a European ambience. I feel lucky to breathe it in.

We both were famished and so we went to McHaley's on Forty-sixth Street and Eighth Avenue. We sat at a booth in the bar area so that Graziela could smoke and we ordered bacon cheeseburgers. For years I was a vegetarian, and before that I was kosher. But of late, I eat almost anything. So this was the first bacon cheeseburger of my life. It was quite decadent and quite good. McHaley's is supposed to have the best burgers on Broadway.

While we ate, I glanced occasionally at the Yankee game on the television. And Graziela smoked—her eating hardly interrupted the flow of cigarettes—and told me her various troubles. I think she believes that because I am a novelist I might know something about life. I haven't disabused her of this notion. And I do know one thing: When someone is in distress the best thing you can do is listen to them, or pretend to listen. Let them drain the wound of their psychic injury and healing takes place. So I listened to Graziela and snuck glances at my heroes, like Bernie Williams and Tino Martinez, on the television.

After our cheeseburgers, which I paid for like a big shot, we strolled through the throngs of Times Square tourists and Graziela launched into a wonderful Mac Wellman monologue. Wellman, a brilliant but somewhat unknown playwright, often utilizes Graziela, and the monologue she performed for me was filled with non sequiturs and baseball references. The Yankee game on the television had inspired her. In her Polish tones, she exclaimed, amidst the Midwesterners and the neon, something Mac Wellmanish, like, "Ball four. I see a cat. Who am I?"

I was a lucky man to have one of New York's great actresses performing for me on Broadway, all for the price of a cheeseburger. Then we went up to her apartment, which is in the Theater District, and her home is like something out of a Tolstoy novel, even though she's Polish. There are hundreds of old beautiful books, lamps with silk shades, gigantic oil paintings, a shiny samovar, black-and-white photos, ladies' hats, tea sets, and because of the lamps, the soft lighted glow of the Old World.

She had me take off my shoes and lie on her large, beautiful daybed. She angled the television in my direction. She wanted to watch me watch the rest of the baseball game. I think it reminded her of her ex-husband, an American who loved baseball. She made us coffee and sat on the other side of the room from me. She smoked and I watched the Yankees.

"I feel like a king," I said, luxuriating in the pillows of the daybed and the freedom of my stocking feet.

"You are a king," she said.

I then asked her to join her king on the daybed but she preferred to sit in her favorite chair. I wanted her next to me so that I could rest my head on her full bosom, but it wasn't meant to be. With women, I am secretly like the baby swan in that children's book who loses his mother and goes around saying, "Are you my mommy?" In my mind I said that to Graziela, but not out loud.

After the Yankee game (another victory, of course), I left Graziela. The Yankees' win had coincided with my digestive process. After the last out, I really needed to use a toilet—Graziela's strong European coffee had activated the bacon cheeseburger, but there was no way I was going to violate Graziela's commode. I'm very neurotic about using other people's toilets. So the end of the game gave me a natural exit, though if I didn't have to go to the bathroom, I probably would have stayed a while longer with the hope that eventually she might have joined me on the daybed. She's over sixty and incredibly sexy. But my toilet issues took precedence over my romantic desires.

In parting, she gave me a tender kiss for each cheek—oh, if there only could have been more!—and I quickly walked over to the Algonquin Hotel to use the bathroom. Since I was in jacket and tie, I knew I wouldn't be harassed. I always like to use the toilets of fancy hotels; it's the closest I come to being a guest.

So I was sitting on the john, feeling the bacon cheeseburger protruding from the area above my pubis like a softball, even though I had just watched a baseball game, and I was concerned. I had been very ready to go and now the thing was stuck. This would be my first and last bacon cheeseburger! I should have remained kosher and vegetarian! I was being punished. I nervously massaged the softball, hoping to force the thing down and out of me. Then the bathroom door opened and I heard a child's voice with an English accent say, "I'll be all right, Daddy." Then an adult English voice said, "I'll be right outside."

And then the stall door next to me was opened and underneath the partition I saw a boy's small, well-clad leather feet. Dear child, I thought. Then he expelled a large, gaseous, noisy multisyllabic fart.

"Oh, pardon," he said, so politely, and his little accent was adorable. But what gas he had. His fart, though, inspired me—the softball made a tectonic move, I created a stink, and I said to the unseen boy, "There's something rotten in the state of Denmark," which is what I often say to myself on the john, but this time I shared it with a fellow gastric sufferer.

The boy didn't respond verbally, but he let loose a bellow of a fart, which seemed to be way out of proportion to his shoe size, and again he said in a high-pitched British whisper befitting Prince Harry, "Oh, pardon."

I wondered what was causing such gas in one so young. I concluded that it must be jet lag—it was after eleven—and unusual American fare. I did so admire his good manners, though. My young son makes no apology when he farts; in fact, he tries to fart *on me* if he can time it correctly.

I finished before the young Brit, and I got out of my stall with a vague sense of guilt for having uttered my Denmark line to the boy. Alone with a child in a public toilet, one shouldn't engage in conversation or quote Shakespeare—anything could be construed as sexual abuse these days. So as I exited the restroom, I glanced at the father with nervous eyes as if I had just raped his son and I walked quickly out to Forty-fourth Street and jogged down to Broadway, fearing a false accusation of pederasty.

With such thoughts on my mind, I decided to go to Edelweiss, my old transsexual hangout, which had been closed down for several months. But I had heard through the transsexual grapevine that the club had reopened, despite Puritan Giuliani's best efforts. But what indignity of decency will be next for New York under this madman? Public squares where perverts are put in wooden stocks? This could backfire, though, on Guiliani, since the S&M crowd would certainly try to get themselves arrested and publicly humiliated.

Anyway, I paid twenty dollars to get into Edelweiss, and I found the place to be a shadow of its former sordid self. They aren't allowed to serve alcohol and there were very few trannies and very few tranny-chasers. And it was a Saturday night! Giuliani has sucked all the life out of Edelweiss. He's driven all the girls to the back pages of the *New York Press* and the *Village Voice*. But it was so much more fun when the trannies had to *go out* to find their clientele. There was intrigue, competition, rivalry, pageantry, and passion. It was a society that flourished. Now everyone's wary and defeated-looking.

But my trip to Edelweiss wasn't a complete disaster. I did spot one girl who was quite exotic and whom I had never seen before. She was an incredibly tiny Filipino, about four foot eight. I bought her a drink and she was so feminine and small that I wondered if she was a real girl masquerading as a transsexual, kind of a reverse Madame Butterfly. Instead of hiding a penis, she'd have to hide the lack of one.

Her name was June, and her hair was long and silky, and her features were altogether girlish, though the Asians do make the best and easiest transition to womanhood, followed by the Latinos, then blacks, and, lastly, whites. I gave June five dollars and we went to a corner of the club, and I sat on a chair and she sat on my lap. I bounced her on my knee and it was quite pleasurable. Her back was to me and I put my face in her smooth black hair; I inhaled her perfume. Up and down she went on my knee, and I didn't know if I was enjoying it because I thought she was a child, a woman, a man, a trans-sexual, or a dwarf. Which perverted impulse of mine was she appealing to?

I wasn't the only one having a good time—she also liked playing horsey on my knee. She liked the presence of my hard-on. She reached back enthusiastically and held on to it like a knob in a Western saddle, and as she happily rode me like a Saratoga jockey, she kept saying, "If you want to know me, call me." She spoke with an interesting Filipino accent and her use of "want to know me" was intriguing. It was a night of unusual language—Graziela performing the Wellman monologue and telling me I was a king, the young English boy with his use of "pardon," and now June with her supplication that I "know her." When she finally got off my knee she gave me her card. She works as a manicurist in Babylon, Long Island. Of course it would be Babylon.

After such a pleasant experience with June, I thought the night could only go downhill, so I figured I had better get out of Edelweiss. "Home, Jeeves," I said to myself, which is what I often say to myself when I should leave Edelweiss, but it only works about a third of the time. Mostly, I don't listen to myself and I stay out much too late, hoping for something interesting to happen, and this can often lead to trouble. For example, there was the time when one of the girls, who had been booted from the place, threw a Molotov cocktail at the front door and we all had to evacuate through some weird underground passage. What if I had died in a fire in a tranny club? My poor parents! Such a death does not look good in one's obituary, and how would my memorial in the *Princeton Alumni Weekly* read? *Jonathan Ames, '87, died in a fire in a New York nightclub known as Edelweiss. Jonathan was on the fencing team and was an English major. . . .* And that was a night when my invoking of Jeeves to take me home had failed!

But the night I bounced June on my knee, I left the club early and got a cab. During the ride home, I stared out the window at New York, and I took particular notice of all the Korean markets with their brightly colored displays of fruits. They were beautiful, but who would eat all those grapefruits and oranges and watermelons? It seemed to me that most people ate poorly and those fruits wouldn't move off the displays, the way one's novel—like my recently published applegreen book, *The Extra Man*—might not move off the shelves of the bookstores. And then I thought how my novel and all the fruits in New York would all go to a terrible waste. I pitied myself and the owners of the Korean markets.

But then I stopped such depressing thoughts and I took stock of my incredible evening. There had been all the interesting language I had heard, a tasty if toxic bacon cheeseburger, Graziela's sexy smoky company, a Yankee victory, the mannered farts of an English schoolboy, and the erotic knee-bouncing of a lovely transsexual dwarf. Perhaps Puritan Giuliani hasn't destroyed this town, after all. Not, at least, if you know where to go, what to do, and how to do it.

1998

In 2004, I was one of many writers who wrote definitions for The Future Dictionary of America. *This book was published by McSweeney's to raise money for progressive organizations and was edited by Dave Eggers, Jonathan Safran Foer, and Nicole Krauss. The directions I received for creating words were the following: "Each writer should use or invent a word (a noun, a verb, an adjective, whatever) for something whose existence would make America a better place. Think of it as a dictionary of language for describing what the future could look like. A dictionary that is both useful and romantic. Hopeful and necessary. Pragmatic and idealistic."*

Throughout I Love You More Than You Know, *you will find the definitions I wrote. They will appear, of course, in alphabetical order.*

Bald-is-beautiful (balled-iz-byoo'te'fel), adj. A description, usually directed at men who have lost a good deal if not all of their hair. What had previously been a somewhat jokey, somewhat consoling remark, meant to soothe the egos of bald men, became an official part of the lexicon in 2009, when it was discovered by beauty scientists at Carleton College in Northfield, Minnesota, that bald is actually beautiful. A statistical analysis of Michael Jordan, the bald American eagle, several million infants, and old movie footage of Yul Brynner in *Westworld* helped lead to this discovery. Further proof was culled from a controlled experiment by the Carleton scientists in which several thousand men with comb-overs had their heads shaved and it was revealed that 78 percent of these formerly mildly unattractive men were now beautiful. The findings of the Carleton study were then confirmed when Donald Trump, a noted financier, real-estate magnate, and New York mayor (2008–14) celebrated for his bad taste and astonishingly freakish comb-over, succumbed to pressure from the UN in 2009 and shaved his comb-over. Images of Trump, which were proliferating around the world due to his election as mayor of the Capital of the Universe, were causing psychotic breaks from reality for fragile people with hair issues and an international health crisis was declared. Once Trump shaved his head, people marveled at how lovely he actually was, and after serving as mayor he began to hang out with the famously bald Dalai Lama, forging a connection between spirituality and the accumulation of wealth that had previously not existed, which benefited a good many people— the poor opened savings accounts and the rich started praying and helping the poor. This gorgeous teaming up of the Dalai and the Donald thus solidified the phrase *bald-is-beautiful* as a full-fledged member of the English language.

RUE ST. DENIS

Prostitution is legal in France, and in Paris there's this long winding street called Rue St. Denis and at night hundreds of prostitutes—some beautiful, some hideous—stand in the doorways waiting for men. At one end of the road is the famous shopping area Les Halles and its ultramodern underground mall, and at the other end of the road is a Romanesque arch built by Louis the 14th—La Porte de St. Denis.

When I lived in Paris in the spring of '89, I would often parade up and down Rue St. Denis. And I was part of an enormous mob—for every prostitute there were four or five men. There were literally thousands of us. We'd spill off the sidewalks, and cars could hardly negotiate their way.

We were like an army; if we'd had a leader we could have accomplished something. But we were all there just silently marching and looking, and all the while weighing our cheapness against our lust: Should I just go home and masturbate for free, or should I spend three hundred francs to be inside a woman who doesn't love me?

At least this is what I was thinking, and I will say that for the most part my cheapness was much more powerful than my lust. But there were other factors as well—fear of disease (even with a condom, I was nervous about germs), the sordidness (the idea that numerous other men that night had already been with the woman, pressing their horrible bodies against her), and my knowledge and experience that being with a prostitute is this sad mimicry of sex with a woman who actually wants you, and that afterward you're disgusted with yourself and half-dead and not only have you killed yourself a little, but you've contributed to the ongoing destruction of another person—the woman who sold you her mouth and breasts and vagina.

So with all these negative factors why was I drawn so many nights, with thumping heart, to stare at and regard the women of Rue St. Denis? First of all, I was only twenty-five and was quite curious, as I still am, about the world, especially the world of sex. Secondly, I have what the Marquis de Sade called *la nostalgie de la boue*—a nostalgia for the mud. Or to put it more simply, I've always been drawn to the gutter; I like the people I meet there. And thirdly, I've never been in possession of great, sustained mental health. And it's been my belief for some time now that most of my sex drive has nothing to do with sex or pleasure—it has to do with insanity. All the troubles in my psyche and my nervous system get filtered through and find expression in my libido.

So mental insanity is the primary reason I was enlisted in the Rue St. Denis army. But there was also a physiological issue—I want on some base level of my being to fornicate with every attractive woman I see. And I don't think this part is insanity, it's biology. But in my lifetime, and I think I speak for most men, I will actually have sex with about .0000001 percent of the women I'd like to have sex with.

Thus, men are drawn to the Rues St. Denis of the world—where every woman we look at we can have. For once repression is lifted. It's an alternative universe. But of course it's not ideal—we have to pay for the women. In our little-boy hearts we'd like the attraction to be reciprocal, but any man who thinks a prostitute wants him for anything other than money is a fool. Of course, there are many such fools. They are the bread and butter of the business.

So all this is to say that one warm spring night as I lurched up and down the Rue, I saw a woman who caused me to overcome my cheapness and my other reservations. She stood alone in her narrow, slanted doorway, and she had long dark hair and she was wearing cat's-eye glasses, which made her look like a schoolteacher. And this was utterly disarming. She was in bra and panties like the others—that's all they usually wore, or a tight dress—and her figure was good, and her face was comely. But it was the glasses. I'd never seen a prostitute with glasses. I approached her. She smiled at me.

"Bonsoir," I said in my American accent.

"*Vous parlez Francais?*" she asked.

"*Oui.*"

But she didn't believe me. She continued in very good English. "Do you want to go upstairs?"

"Yes."

She took my hand, like a mother leading a child, and

there was a tender, gentle look on her face. I was hers without any resistance. She took me through the doorway, and my legs felt weak from excitement and the transgression of my actions. We climbed a dirty wooden staircase. Another prostitute, on her way down, passed us.

At each landing there were two doors, and the building was ancient and felt like it could collapse at any moment—the floors and the staircase were warped, tilting. At the fifth floor, she unlocked a door. Inside was a sink, a narrow bed with a metal frame, a bureau, and a chair. And there was a single window with thin curtains. I looked out the window. Down below I could see the men marching. She asked for the money. I gave it to her. She put it in her little purse. And in the light of the room, she looked older than she had on the street. She was in her late thirties or early forties.

She undressed me, and put my clothes neatly on the chair. There was a single sheet on the bed. She took a towel from the bureau and laid it on the sheet. I sat naked on the towel. Then she took a small towel that was by the sink and she wet it. She sat next to me and washed my penis. It felt good, but I wondered about the wet towel—it was clearly unsanitary, used by her on other men. And the towel I was sitting on was also probably covered with germs. But I let it all go. She washed the tops of my thighs.

"This must be a difficult life," I said, and I said this because I am an idiot. Even as I sin I want forgiveness.

She looked at me quizzically. I repeated myself in French.

"It's not a difficult life," she said, answering in English. "I only work a few nights. And I don't live in Paris—it's too expensive. In my town I can send my children to very good schools."

"How many children do you have?"

"Three," she said.

I was in a Balzac story. My prostitute was a mother of three. She took off her bra and panties. Her breasts sagged. There were folds of flesh in her belly as she bent to remove her heels. Then she took off the glasses. A terrible mistake. But I was too embarrassed to ask her to put them back on. I didn't want to seem abnormal.

She took a condom from her purse and she had us lie down on the towel. She masturbated me a little, then put the condom on me. She made a joke about my reddish pubic hair. She had a thick patch of dark hair. Then she shifted me on top of her and I couldn't get it in. The bed was sinking, making it difficult to penetrate. She pulled her legs back, but I started losing my erection. I touched her breast for inspiration and she provided the obligatory fake moan. The nipple was thick and brown. I thought of her three children. I couldn't get it in. I looked at the glasses on the bureau. Should I ask her? My erection was wilting. Three hundred francs wasted. Then she grabbed hold of it and squeezed the blood into it and guided me in her and as soon as I was in I came. I tried to throw in a few fake thrusts. But she knew. I rolled off her. At least it was over. She took the condom off me and washed me again with the towel.

She put on her lingerie and I got dressed. Then she put on her glasses and that made me want to try again, even though it would cost another three hundred francs.

"I like your glasses," I said, shyly, which was to be my lead-in to asking her to keep them on and to suggest we have another go.

"Thank you," she said. "Many men like them." She smiled. She knew they were a lure. I wished she had worn them when we lay down, but I decided not to ask if we could try again. She walked to the door of the room and opened it for me to leave. But not in a mean way. There was nothing mean about her. She had only been kind to me.

I stood at the door. "*Merci*," I said.

"You're welcome," she said. No one in Paris would speak French with me. Then she gave me a kiss on the cheek—the first kiss exchanged between us—and locked the door behind me. She was going to stay in the room and clean up a little.

I hurried down the stairs and when I hit the street I started running. I ran past all the whores and whoremongers. I ran all the way home—about two miles—through beautiful Paris. I was running like I had committed a crime. I felt this way even though in France prostitution is legal.

1998

TROUBLES WITH
COCKROACHES AND
YOUNG GIRLS

Like many people, I use the first bathing experience of the day to clear my nose. But because I take baths—I don't have a shower, only this tiny tub in my kitchen—the buildup in my nostrils doesn't disappear down a drain; it swirls in my bathwater with all my other chafings and scrapings and water-soluble detritus. I try to keep an eye out for the mucus, to make sure it doesn't get tangled in my leg hair, but usually it just disappears and then I try to forget about the whole thing. I try to forget how humiliating it is to have a body.

But the other morning, I had another bad incident in my tub. This time I didn't scald my testicles, like I did a few months ago, but I blew my nose and an interesting sculpture came out with some dark blood in it. It floated down by my feet and I felt sickened by my grotesque existence, and then I didn't see the mucus anymore, it must have sank, and so I engaged in my usual amnesia, pretending that nothing had happened.

I continued bathing and worked on my scalp with my rubber invigorator—my hair seems to be doing better lately—and then I saw the mucus on my ankle. This is disgusting! I thought. I can't stand it! Why is life so ridiculous?

And then the mucus moved. Was my bathwater swirling because of the rotation of the earth and it had shifted the mucus? Then the mucus reversed directions. What kind of mucus was this to defy the spinning of the planet? Then I realized, with my Ivy League–trained mind, that this wasn't snot. It was a cockroach! In my tub! On my ankle! This was worse than Kafka!

I shrieked and momentarily left my body. I astrally projected myself onto the ceiling, and I wondered as I heard myself screaming if this time my neighbors might take an interest in my wailing—at least once every two weeks I scream in terror about something—but, as always, there was no knock at the door. I have at least eight neighbors along my hallway and they've never responded to my cries. Granted I'm always crying wolf—scalded testicles, splinters, shaving nicks, insane phone bills, sharklike cockroaches—but they don't know that. If a serial killer with a taste for writers climbs into my window via the fire escape, I'm a dead man. New York is a lonely town.

Anyway, after I screamed for about five seconds, which is pretty long for a scream, I returned to this world and thrashed my ankle and the cockroach fell into the water. Then I leaped out of the tub before the cockroach swam into my cock, like those fish I've heard about in the Amazon, and I imagine a cockroach might do such a thing to a cock since they share the same first name.

So I stood there dripping on the kitchen floor and the cockroach was scrambling up the side of the tub, coming after me, and I took a dish from the sink and pushed him down into the bathwater. Then I bravely and heroically plunged my hand into the water and undid the plug. A small whirlpool began—the earth's rotation was now properly asserting itself—and I watched the cockroach's death struggle (not without sympathy, mind you) until the poor creature disappeared down the drain. It's horrible to watch anything die, even a cockroach that has tried to kill you. But I moved on and I thoroughly rinsed the tub of cockroach germs and got back in—I still had soap in my thinning hair.

Cleaned up, I got dressed and headed out for some morning coffee. But it was around noon, a late start. Such is the life of a starving writer. My own hours. Very little pay, but a good schedule. I walked down Third Street and the kids were in recess at the local school, playing on their playground.

I moved along the fence that keeps the children safe from passersby, and a young girl, maybe eight, was pressing her face against the metal links, like a prisoner. She was stunningly beautiful. Light brown hair, flawless skin, green eyes.

And as I looked at this young girl, she smiled at me fetchingly. And there was a look in her eye that seemed to indicate a carnal knowledge beyond her years. My warped mind happily thought: She's attracted to me. So I winked at her.

Then my rational mind exploded: What am I doing, winking like that? Am I mad, perverted? Do I want to traumatize the child?

I scurried down to Avenue A before one of the teachers could call the police. I turned the corner and blended in with the sidewalk traffic. As I walked, I analyzed my actions, and I was reminded of an incident years before: I was in New Jersey and was taking my dog for a walk and as I came around a bend in the road, a woman, about twenty-five yards away, was standing by her car. When she saw me, she began to wave at me happily. My instantaneous thought was: Does she want to sleep with me?

As I eagerly approached her, it was apparent that the car had a flat tire, and she wanted my help. Nothing more. I described this incident to a friend and he said that in that moment when I thought the woman wanted me for sex simply because she was waving at me captured perfectly the sad essence of the male condition. We are desperate, he explained, for any sign of approval from women, and we will misread the slightest friendly gesture as an entreaty to copulation.

But as I walked down Avenue A, feeling like Peter Lorre in *M*, I took no solace in my recollection of my friend's theory. It was one thing for me to misinterpret women, but another thing for me to misinterpret a young girl. I was concerned that with my wink I had destroyed a clean record when it came to child molesting. I have lots of problems, but I've never had a thing for children.

What was I to do? I needed coffee. I doubled back on Avenue A and I made the mistake of going into the Limbo cafe—it was filled with writers at their laptops writing screen-plays. It was like an old Hollywood studio. And where do these people get their money to sit in cafes all day and write? I have no money but I stay alone in my apartment, which is where people with no money should be, not out in the world flaunt-ing it. And, furthermore, how can they write in public? I need to do it privately so that I can nervously fondle myself every few sentences.

I used to write in cafes, but only in journals, and by hand. I'd write of my loneliness, and I'd hope that a woman would look over my shoulder and read my journal and fall in love with me. It was romantic. All these laptops, though, have turned cafes into offices.

But the vice squad was after me for my wink, I needed to get off the streets, so I went up to the counter and ordered a coffee. Then I sat down next to a screenwriter, who was smoking a cigarette and blowing his exhaust right into my face. But I didn't say anything. I deserved the smoke for having traumatized that child. Then I felt a nudging in my groin. I looked under the table. The screenwriter had a dog with him. An attractive husky with blue eyes.

"Can I pet your dog?" I asked. The screenwriter nodded his head, and I discreetly glanced at his computer as he typed a line of dialogue: "Fuck you."

I didn't know if this was meant for me, or was merely a Mamet/Tarantino influence. So before the screenwriter took back his permission, I put my head under the table and nuzzled my face into his dog's neck. I had a few moments of gratify-ing anonymous love. I'm not a pedophile, but I do have a thing for dogs.

Then the dog went for someone else's crotch, and I did feel a little jealous, I have to admit. I'm very possessive when it comes to dogs—I want them to love only me, which is absurd. I sort of feel the same way about lesbians. I don't want them to like women; I want them to like men, and by extension, like me. If I met a lesbian with a dog it would be a strange double whammy.

So the screenwriter tapped away and I sipped my coffee. I thought things over and I reasoned that the young girl wouldn't really be damaged by my wink. Many adults wink at children, I told myself, and then I thought how kindly Irish priests in the movies always wink at young ragamuffins, and a brief, possibly incorrect, vision of Spencer Tracy in a clerical collar flashed across my mind-screen. Hadn't he played a priest who winked at children? If Spencer Tracy winks at children, it's okay behavior.

Then I thought that Catholic priests weren't a good role model for my winking, considering all the rumors one hears about priests and children, confirmed by the occasional scandal.[1] And I always wonder: Why are they so nuts for young children? Traditionally they go for altar boys, but girls are also sometimes their objects of desire. The whole thing is really a mystery. Priests are so good when it comes to charitable deeds and so terrible when it comes to the most offensive sexual crimes. Do they go into the Church because of their demons, hoping to repress them through prayer and kindly actions, or do the job and the celibacy require-

[1] This was written in the quasi-innocent year of 1998 before all the troubles with the Catholic Church and abusive priests came out in the open.

ment somehow create such demons? Regardless, they are really tormented. No wonder they're always talking about the agony and the ecstasy. I will say that the pope seems to be well-behaved, but I think he's the exception and not the rule.

Anyway, Limbo was getting to me—all the cigarette smoke and screenwriting—so I took my coffee and got out of there. I walked back past the playground, returning to the scene of my crime. All guilty people, if they have any morality, want to be caught and punished—that's why they go back. The children were still outside. I looked for the girl, but I couldn't spot her. I hoped that she was all right.

The weather was unusually mild and some boys were playing baseball. They were using a tennis ball and an aluminum bat. I was glad to see they wanted to play our dying national pastime, but the boy at bat swung wildly and almost brained the catcher. This alarmed me. I was a lifeguard in my late teens and ever since that time I am upset by reckless behavior. I was always frightened when the kids would run around the pool. I'd blow my lifeguard whistle to no avail, and I'd envision them slipping and cracking open their skulls.

So I called out to a teacher, who wasn't paying close enough attention to the dangers of the ball game. "Excuse me, ma'am," I said. "But you should watch these boys. Somebody could be hurt with that bat."

The woman, a tiny exhausted brunette, looked at me with annoyance. "Don't worry," she said curtly. "I'm watching."

I walked home. I had redeemed myself for the wink by possibly saving one of the ballplayers. A good deed cancels out a bad deed. Even if she was annoyed by me, the teacher would keep a closer eye on things and no one would get brain-damaged.

I went up to my apartment to write and fondle myself. As I sat at my desk, I glanced at the aluminum baseball bat left behind by the previous tenant. He had kept it around for clubbing intruders.

I grabbed the bat and got into my old Little League stance. The boys on the playground had inspired me. I took a few swings and pretended to be a Hall of Famer. Then I saw a cockroach crawling on the wall. I couldn't believe it. City life is disgusting. One encounters more nature here than living in the country. I watched the thing move. Was this the cockroach who had attacked me in the tub? Had he somehow survived the drain and climbed back out? Or was it an avenging relative?

I took a mighty swing at the cockroach and missed. I was always lousy at baseball. Plaster fell. My one precious painting crashed to the floor. Its glass casing broke. The painting ripped a little! I screamed. I waited. There was no knock at the door.

I saw the cockroach on the floor, crawling out from under some plaster. He was a hardy little thing. I raised my bat. I had him in my sights. I chopped down. I missed. The bat ricocheted off the floor and into my shin. I howled. I waited. Still no knock. "Doesn't anyone in this building give a shit if I'm dying in here?" I shouted.

Silence was my answer.

1998

MY WIENER IS DAMAGED!

My son came up for his winter visit.[2] What a good kid. And what a big kid. He's twelve and a half years old, but he looks sixteen. He's five foot nine and weighs one hundred and fifty-five pounds. I've got three inches on him, but he's got five pounds on me.

I met him at the airport the day after Christmas. Didn't embarrass him with a hug. Just rubbed his shoulder and shook his hand and said, "You look great. You're huge!" He smiled shyly, happily. I last saw him in October, and in only two months, he had grown an inch and thinned out some, losing more of his baby fat, getting rangy.

I drove him to my parents' house, where I do most of my parenting, in an odd setup where I'm both a son and a

---

[2] In 1987, when I was twenty-three, I found out that I had a fifteen-month-old son. I entered his life and became his dad, seeing him as often as I could.

father. My son stays in my old room, now his room, and I stay in my sister's old room, which is filled with my boxes of rough drafts and manuscripts, old letters, journals, and photos. My whole life history. I'd like to organize it all someday. But I don't know if I have the patience. Or the courage. All those pictures and letters and journals scare me and sadden me. Lost love, lost friends, lost time.

Waiting in my son's room was my gift for him. What he had asked for. A color GameBoy. I had gone all over the city, two days before the 25th, to find one and everywhere I went they were sold out. I was despairing that I would let my son down, but then a Wiz on Broadway received a shipment just as I arrived and I was in luck.

He was really pleased with it and thanked me. He had brought some of his game cartridges up from Georgia and he put them in and began to play immediately. He loved the new sleeker design and the enhanced color—his old GameBoy was black and white. He wanted me to try and I gave it a go at Donkey Kong, but I wasn't too good, though holding that thing reminded me of my little handheld football game that I loved back in my freshman year of high school. I mastered it and would try to set personal records for touchdowns, kind of like my addiction to computer solitaire in adulthood. All the kids in my high school had the football game, but actually they had the high-priced version—my dad had bought for me a cheaper imitation kind that was a little different. So I could never compare my scores with the other kids, which wasn't so great, because at lunchtime that was part of the fun, to compete with one another. I had asked my father for the game that everyone had, but he had assured me that the cheaper version was just as good, and I couldn't articulate to him why it wasn't.

I received a lot of love growing up—I had a fine childhood. Still, it probably screwed me up a little—like in the case of the football game—that my father would almost never buy me anything brand-name or new, even though we were squarely middle class in a middle-class town. My father, you see, was raised in the Depression with very little and was unable to exorcise himself of the mentality of that time, which is understandable to me now, but was less so when I was a child.

My first baseball mitt was one my father found in a garbage can in Brooklyn in the 1950s, and he held on to it for years, waiting until he had a son. It was a dried-up old first baseman's mitt and he said I could get a new one when I learned how to catch, but you couldn't catch with that thing. It's a terrible pun, but this was a real catch-22. How could I learn to snare a baseball with such a mitt? I was lucky the coach put me in left field and that no one at that age could hit the ball in the air. By the time the balls reached me, they were rolling, and I picked up the grounders with my bare hand.

My great-aunt, ever my savior, seeing that lousy mitt, was the one who bought me a new one my second year in baseball, and I loved and worshiped the new Rawlings glove she got me.

And since I'm being a self-pitying baby, I'll complain here that I never had a new bike or new baseball cleats or new ice skates. We lived on a lake, which pre—global warming was frozen from December to February, and I skated quite a lot and would have loved a new pair of hockey skates like the other kids. But my dad would always take me to this secondhand sports shop and I'd get this strange, used stuff, which was always a source of embarrassment. I had odd bikes, odd skates, odd cleats. But at least I got stuff, so I can't really complain, though I'm managing to do so anyway.

The point of all this is that now, as an adult, I can hardly buy anything for myself. I have a phobia about it. Buying something for my son or for a girlfriend, I have no problem, I could care less about the money, but to purchase something for myself is nearly impossible. I must not think I deserve something new, coupled with a tremendous, inherited fear of spending money. The expenditure of money during my childhood was so associated with pain and gravitas that I'm now paralyzed as an adult. Granted, I don't have much money in the first place, but what little I have, I can never spend.

My self-stinginess manifests itself in many different ways. For example, you're supposed to switch toothbrushes every two months, but I do it more like every two years, and even then I usually steal one from my mother's stash. It's disgusting: I brush my teeth with bacteria every night. Instead of cleaning my teeth, I'm making them worse, and, furthermore, I haven't been to a dentist in years due to the cost and not having health insurance, which I can't afford anyway.

I recently got a new pair of shoes, but I had to build up my courage for about a year. I kept walking past this store on the corner of First Avenue and St. Marks, intently eyeballing the window display, until one day I just burst in there and got a pair before I knew what had happened.

And then when I do get something new, like my shoes, I sort of worship my purchase for some time, admiring its beauty, and have to ask my friends repeatedly, "Do you like my new shoes?" I ask this fully expecting that they'll all say yes, but I'm compelled to ask because I'm so proud of my new thing and want it to be praised. Sometimes, though, like a body adjusting to an organ transplant, it takes me a while to trust a new piece of clothing, to accept it into my little wardrobe family.

Two and a half years ago, this girlfriend of mine was disgusted by the underwear I had on. It was all shredded and stained—I'd had the same seven pairs for over a decade. My fear of spending money had kept me in these repulsive rags, but this woman couldn't take it and she bought me two pairs of underwear from the Gap. And they felt so good that I went into a Gap by myself—I had never been in one before; almost all my clothing comes from thrift shops or is given to me as gifts from my great-aunt or my mother—and I discovered that lots of underwear was for sale. Every month, the Gap changes its styles and you can get really nice boxer shorts—last month's styles—for just a few bucks.

So I went on a rampage of underwear-buying and now I'm up to about ten pairs. And I've been so happy about having new underwear that at one of my Fez shows, I brought all my Gap underwear onstage and threw them in the air. It was meant to be an expression of joy—all the colors of my boxers glittering in the lights and me dancing about as they fell around me. I was acting like some kind of spring faerie or wood nymph, but I wasn't really acting. I was truly happy. In fact, this underwear thing has gone so well that I recently bought a new toothbrush, and I just love it. Even as I write this self-pitying essay, I may slowly be getting better.

Anyway, after my son and I played with his brand-new, brand-name GameBoy,[3] we drove to this state park to hike up a mountain. Where I grew up in New Jersey, there's this little mountain range called the Ramapos, and my son and I have a couple of different spots where we like to go for long walks.

As we went up the trail, he told me all about his latest passions—WWF[4] wrestling and his hero, the wrestler Stone Cold Steve Austin. He kept repeating Austin's signature phrase, "And that's the bottom line, because Stone Cold said so." My son gave me a total education on the WWF—the different rivalries and characters, the good guys and the bad. We also, during our discussion, made our usual fart noises and fart jokes and sometimes hid behind trees to act like spies when we saw other hikers approaching.

We were getting along great, and I was relieved. I had been a little concerned about this visit. When I had seen him in October, down in Georgia, we had a good time, but there was a distance there that had never been present before. I was scared that adolescence was really settling in and that I was losing him. The phone calls over the next two months were also marked by what felt like an unspoken barrier.

But over this eight-day winter visit, beginning with that hike, my son was incredibly happy and laughed continually. We were very close, which was much different from our time

---

[3] Nietzsche wrote: "In your children you shall make up for being the children of your father; thus you shall redeem all that is past." My father has been great to me and I adore him, but in this one area of buying something new and brand-name for my son, this Nietzsche quote applies.
[4] Now known as the WWE.

together in October. And I think that visit was strange because I went down to his world, and I hadn't been there for over a year and a half—he mostly comes to me, about every six to eight weeks. But he had wanted me to come down to see his bicycle: a beautiful BMX that he had spent months and months assembling with all the best parts and which he keeps in pristine condition.

So I went to Georgia, and while there were no incidents or problems, I think in his more mature eyes, he saw clearly how I don't fit into his life down there. For so many years, my son had wanted me to live with him, to marry his mother, but in October he must have finally seen that this dream can never come true and so he was quiet and withdrawn. I had thought it was the beginning of sullen adolescence, but I think it was this other thing—a more mature understanding of what he can never have, and the subsequent sadness.

But up here, he was his old, buoyant self again. With him, I'm part father, part older brother, and part comedian. And I must let him down in a hundred thousand ways, but if nothing else I make him laugh. I just have to look at him and he cracks up. When he arrived, he was kind of pimply, but by the end of the visit his skin had really cleared up. I think it might have been all the laughing.

After our hike that first day, we came back to the house and my mother laid out a Jewish deli meal. My son likes to have "Jewish food" when he sees his grandparents, the Jewish side of his blood. So my mother started us off with chicken soup with matzo balls, followed by corned beef, pastrami, and hot dogs. There was also some salad, which my fiber-conscious mind was grateful for. At one point, I went over to the stove to fork a hot dog and as I walked back to the table I held the frankfurter in front of my crotch and drawled like a madman, "Oh, no, I forked my wiener. Help! Help! Help!" My son cracked up, and it did look funny, this kosher frank emerging from the front of my pants zipper, impaled by a fork.

"My wiener is damaged! My wiener is damaged!" I bellowed. My son was now in hysterics—he had to spit out a mouthful of masticated corn beef; thank God he didn't choke—and my mother was shouting, "Why can't we have a nice meal!?!" My father looked up from his plate and he seemed to be mildly amused—there was a twinkle in his strange eyes—and I have to say that just as I am improving somewhat about money, so has my father. When it comes to my son and to me, my father spares no money or love. He has bailed me out repeatedly as I struggle to make it as a writer, and without both my parents I could not be a father to my son. Well, I could be, but they make it so much better and easier. I'm incredibly lucky the way they support me and love me. It may all sound very sentimental, but it's true, and sometimes in life you have to be sentimental. That's why the word is in the dictionary.

Anyway, while standing next to the kitchen table, I put the wiener, still attached to my crotch, onto my plate, and said in my madman voice, "I'll just use this knife to hold down my wiener and pull out this fork." I then pinned the wiener to the plate with my knife and yanked out the fork, but the knife cut off the head and I screamed, "Oh, my God, I cut off the head! Mommy! Daddy! Help me! Somebody put that thing on ice. Call 911. Get the ice! Call 911. My wiener must be saved!"

"You're insane," said my son, his puberty-addled voice cracking, his eyes watering, "you're sick!" But he was smiling happily and laughing hysterically and my parents were laughing, too. Then I calmed down and we all resumed eating. And the rest of the visit was more or less like that.

So by making my son laugh, the best gift I can give him, I must redeem some of the past, as Nietzsche said, although there's much I can't and don't do for my son. But that will give him something to work on if he ever has children. I can take solace in that.

1998

Humanofuel (hyoo'man'o-fyoo-el), n. A source of energy, supplied by human beings. An overweight but exceedingly clever scientist at Ohio University by the name of Max Odzer discovered *humanofuel* in 2012. During the obesity plague of 2011, which struck the entire Midwest, Max, like thousands of countless others, was legally forced to go to a gym by the government. It was while running on a treadmill that Max realized there was untapped potential in all this exercising. He then created the Odzer-Generator, which was attached to gyms all over America and soon all over the world. While people exercised on treadmills, bicycles, and other strange devices, the Odzer-Generator took this wind-and-water-millesque energy and converted it into *humanofuel,* i.e., power, which then provided electrical and heating energy to the surrounding neighborhoods for each gym and charged batteries for electrical cars. The world, almost overnight, became a better place—people were fit, pollution and global warming were eradicated, sportswear stocks skyrocketed, and everyone, by exercising, was being a good citizen. Max was awarded a Nobel Prize and his waistline went from a 54 to a 32.

I CALLED MYSELF EL CID

In my youth, I was something of a swordsman. I'm not saying I was a great lover, because I wasn't. I had a real problem with misfiring. I was overwhelmed, you see, by the female. What I would do back then is string together three or four premature ejaculations and hope that it added up to a satisfying session for the young lady. Now-a-days, of course, I would be quite proud of myself if I could get it up three times in a night. How life changes.

Anyway, when I say I was a swordsman, I mean an actual swordsman—a fencer. My sophomore year at Princeton, 1983–84, I was the captain of the sabre-squad of the fencing team. I was a fit athlete and in the flower of youth. My teammates and I practiced every afternoon for three hours, but in the early morning, around six a.m., I would have private lessons from the Coach, who was a former French Commando. He was bald, somewhat insane, and bore a passing resemblance to Sean Connery. I admired him terribly.

Up and down the floor of the fencing room, during our morning sessions, he'd come at me with a thick lead bar instead of a sabre, swinging it at me, forcing me to defend myself.

"Pull your balls in," he'd say. "Create a band of steel from the hips down."

"Yes, Coach," I'd say and I would suck in my balls and go down deeper into my *en garde* position. And he'd keep coming at me with that heavy lead bar as I retreated. He'd swing the bar at my ribs and I would parry it with the guard of my sabre. There would be a great clang of metal and then I would riposte—return with my counterattacks: chops to his mask, slashes across his belly, cuts to his rib cage, and slices down his shoulders. He would wear the thick leather suit of a coach so that I wouldn't raise welts on his body. And he was using the lead bar to make me strong, inviolable.

"Commando," he'd say every few minutes to urge me on, to keep me fighting.

We would do this three times a week, just he and I alone, no one else from the team. It was my special commando training to turn me into a warrior on the fencing strip. The Coach had fought in the French-Algerian war, and he believed in fitness and combat even more than most fencing coaches. He was in his early fifties, but was still in trim, fighting shape.

After my morning lesson, we'd sit in his office and cool down. My legs would be swollen and exhausted—from fencing you develop incredibly muscular thighs and calves, since in the *en garde* position you are always crouching, always maintaining your groin in a band of steel. I would drink some water and the Coach, his beautiful bald head glistening with sweat, would regale me with long-winded war tales from his days in Algeria. He often told me this one story—perhaps because of battle trauma he was somewhat repetitive.

"We were making our way through this little village, which we had seized," he would say. "We were checking the buildings for snipers. I was carrying my rifle, of course. Always ready. Always alert. But then suddenly there was a great searing pain in my buttocks. I've been shot, I thought. But then I realized I was flying through the air. I was twenty feet off the ground; I saw my men below me. Was it a mortar? No—it was an electric cable that had come undone, and it had whipped through the air and bit me like a black snake. I got over a thousand volts and so I was flying. But I landed, like a cat, on my feet, ready to fight. I was a Commando."

* * *

When I'd leave the Coach, I'd jog slowly back to my dorm, furthering my conditioning. Then, in my room, I'd do one hundred push-ups, even though my right arm was aching from parrying the Coach's lead bar. I was driving myself like this because I was bent on revenge. I wanted to defeat all my opponents, but I had become fixated most of all on destroying the number one sabre fencer at Columbia—George Leary. He'd been beating me in national competitions when we were both in high school, and he had continued his dominance our first year in college. In more than a dozen bouts, I had never beaten him. But now, in my sophomore year, 1983, I wanted his head. I wasn't going to lose to him again.

What had made his reign over me so dreadful was that he was not an athlete. He was chubby and his face was pasty. He would whine to the judges during his bouts, and then politic with them afterward. And on the fencing strip, he was savvy and tricky, not graceful. He grew up in New York City and before attending Columbia he had studied with a famous exiled Hungarian sabre master and had learned many exotic moves. So even though Leary was fat and ignoble, he was unbeatable, one of the best in the country. Also, he had snubbed me once at a party at the Junior Olympics in 1981 in Cleveland. Claimed to have forgotten my name. I hated George Leary.

The meet against Columbia was scheduled for late February. The season began in November and I trained hard all those months. And in practice every afternoon, I, as the weapon-leader, challenged my sabre squad to keep up with me. I gave them all nicknames—Sir Gawain, Green Knight, Black Knight, Lancelot, Don Quixote—and myself I called El Cid. Don Quixote, a lumbering freshman, bore a passing resemblance to Leary, and I would take great pleasure in bruising his ribs and leaving welts across his ample belly.

Against the other teams—the Penns and Yales and Harvards—I was doing very well, winning three quarters of all my bouts. But I was always aiming toward my confrontation with my Columbia nemesis. The school newspaper, the *Princetonian*, caught wind of my nickname and would dutifully report that Jonathan "El Cid" Ames had thoroughly vanquished his opponents. And along with my pretentious nickname, I tended to be theatrical on the fencing strip. I was very much caught up in the myth of sword fighting, and whenever I struck my foes I would scream in French, "*Et laaa!*" which sounded like "Aye lah!" French is the language of fencing—all its terms are Gallic—and "*Et la!*" is often shouted by fencers; it means "And there!" as in "And there! Take that, you swine." I just happened to scream "*Et la!*" louder than most.

Two days before the big Columbia meet it was unusually warm, and I took my sabre squad out to our ancient football field, Palmer Stadium. I had us climb to the top of the bleachers, and then over a wall. At the very top, the stadium was surrounded with what looked like the battlements of a castle. I had us duel up there, and we engaged in a dangerous free-for-all. I drove my teammates to the edge of the battlements, slashing at them like Errol Flynn.

Finally, the day of the Columbia meet arrived. We took a bus to New York and I sat next to the Coach for part of the ride. He told me more war stories to put me in the right frame of mind. Like myself, he was particularly anxious for a victory against the Lions. We were the underdogs, and this fueled the Coach's commando spirit. Also, he and the Columbia coach had once been romantic rivals for the affection of a certain lady, and so the lingering affects of this old romantic triangle added to the drama and pathos of the whole thing, which is what sex will always do. Add drama and pathos, that is. In short, the Coach wanted to win. He wanted *me* to win.

*   *   *

When we got to the gym, the Columbia team was nowhere to be seen. We started warming up and suddenly the room was filled with music—Wagner's eerie "Ride of the Valkyries." Then the Columbia team raced into the gym, all of them resplendent in their white uniforms, waving their weapons above their heads, and they circled us. And all the while Wagner's horrible music played. It was very impressive—someone on the Columbia team must have been a Drama major.

The meet began. In fencing there are three weapons: foil, épée, and sabre. In foil only the blunt tip of the blade is used and the target area is the torso. In épée, like foil, only the tip is used, but the whole body is the target. And in sabre one can use the tip, but the primary way to score is to cut and slash. The target area is everything above the waist, including the head and the hands.

We had our opening rounds of all three weapons. In my first bout, I faced the number two Columbia sabre man and I lost. I was too hyped up about Leary. Then the second round came, and as a team we were behind and needed a victory. I was scheduled to face Leary. The moment had arrived. Before going on the strip for my bout, I asked a teammate on the épée squad to punch me in the face. He was a strong fellow who had attended a Texas military high school, and he gave me a really good shot to the cheekbone—a little too hard, actually. But it got my blood racing, and I put on my mask and went out to face my enemy.

As per custom, at the start of the bout, I saluted Leary by bringing my sabre to my mask, and then I saluted the director. Bouts are refereed by a director who determines which fencer has initiated the attack and which fencer has scored. He watches keenly to see if one's blows land or are parried. When I was fencing, the sabre blades were not yet electronically rigged up, unlike foil and épée, and so the director was aided by four judges. This made sabre fencing at the time the least modern and also the most exciting; it was the closest thing to real dueling.

The director was a Holocaust survivor and a legendary person in the fencing world. He was bald and had a strange lump on his forehead. With his German accent, he began the bout by saying in French, "*Allez!*"

Leary and I began our dance, moving back and forth. The first one to score five touches would win. I was deep in my crouch, my band of steel keeping my balls in and lowering my center of gravity so that I could spring out and kill him. I scored the first touch by feinting to his head and then cutting his exposed ribs. Then I scored the second touch with a beautiful riposte to his head. I was up 2–0, and with each touch I would scream, "*Et laaa!*" Then we exchanged touches and I was up 3–1. Leary rallied and tied me, 3–3. Everyone in the gym, about two hundred Columbia fans, were watching our bout and cheering against me. My teammates were shouting, "Go, El Cid!"

I went ahead 4–3 by chasing Leary down the strip and then executing a beautiful flèche with an attack to his shoulder. (Flèche means "arrow," and it's when you literally leap at your opponent, both feet going in the air, so that ideally you appear like an arrow.) Then Leary parried my next attack and cut me across the arm with his riposte. It was tied 4–4. The next touch would end the bout; when you are at 4–4, the director calls it *La Belle,* because the next touch is the beautiful touch, the final touch, and in real dueling the equivalent would be the death blow.

The Coach called time-out and came on the strip. He gave me advice in French, and I was too frantic and mad to understand a word of it. However, I nodded as if I did, so he walked away from me, but then he turned and looked at me with his cool gray eyes and said under his breath, "Commando."

I felt like the electric cable had struck me in the ass—I assumed my *en garde* position, I tightened my band of steel. "*Allez!*" commanded the director. Leary came after me, and pushed me to the end of the strip. I sensed he was going to try his patented attack to cut my left arm. But if I overcompensated with my parry he would then deftly cut my right arm. I waited for him and then he sprang—he was quick and deadly when he needed to be. I met his blade. I didn't overcompensate. The clang of metal was astounding—I had him parried. He was mine. He was off-balance and his head was only a foot from our locked blades. All I had to do was move my sabre efficiently and directly to his mask and for once I would beat him. But then something primitive happened to me—I reared my arm back like a man lifting an axe over his head to chop wood, and this was foolish; it left me exposed. But Leary didn't react and so I brought my blade down on his head with tremendous force and my blade snapped in two. I saw silver glistening in the air as the severed portion went over the hysterical crowd. But it counted—I had broken my blade over his head—and I was bellowing, "*ET LAAAA!!!*"

Leary was woozy, and I was so passionate that I was pumping my now jagged, dangerous sabre up and down. And later I was told that it looked as if I was going to run Leary through. His father, who had paid for all those lessons with the Hungarian master, was shouting irrationally, "His blade is broken! His blade is broken!"

But I didn't stab Leary, and the ancient director with the odd lump on his forehead shouted above all the screaming and said, "Touch to the left, to Princeton!"

And my teammates lifted me up and I shouted again, "*Et la!*" It was the most glorious moment of my athletic career. And then, from my teammates' shoulders, I looked down and saw Leary. His mask was off; his hair was matted with sweat. I reached out my hand and said graciously, "Good bout." I hardly meant it, but it was the right thing to do, and Leary shook my hand. Then my teammates carried me off. I had actually won when I wanted to—that never happens in real life!

When my teammates lowered me, the Coach, maintaining his commando-like dignity, calmly shook my hand, but I could see that his cool eyes were quite happy.

*   *   *

A few years ago at a dinner party, I reenacted this story using my steak knife as a substitute sabre. A woman at the party said she knew George Leary. She later got in touch with him and when she recounted my story, he claimed not to remember me.

1999

RON GOSPODARSKI

This essay was written for Gear *magazine, which has since gone out of business. The magazine had a column about people with unusual jobs, and I was assigned Ron Gospodarski. I interviewed him one afternoon and then wrote this piece in his "voice," as if he had written it, which is how the magazine wanted the column to run. I met Ron in his modest Queens, New York, home. He was friendly and articulate.*

I have a master's in business, but I clean up the aftermath of people's deaths. I run my own company, Bio-Recovery Corporation, which specializes in this. Some people say we profit off death, and in a way that's true, but who would do what we do? One time I was cleaning up a shotgun suicide. There was blood on the floor, bed, ceiling, everywhere. The cops had left behind the brain and part of the skull. The brain was all puffy.

Behind the brain was an extension cord, which I had to move. I moved the cord and it touched the brain just a little and in thirty seconds the whole brain collapsed, like the air went out of it, but then thousands of maggots came gushing out. Imagine if the family had to see that. Their son. Their loved one. We're a business, and sure we want to make a profit, but we do this primarily because we want to help people.

For twenty years I was a paramedic, and people were always asking me, Who can we get to clean this up? And I didn't have an answer for them. Bio-recovery is a fairly new field, and three years ago, I wanted to go into business and I was searching the Internet and I saw that people were doing this—cleaning up death scenes—and so I started my company here in New York City and my sister runs our operation in Buffalo, New York. You'll find most people in this field are former policemen, firemen, or paramedics.

So in this business we deal with homicides, suicides, industrial accidents, any kind of violent death, also natural deaths. We save families the pain of having to deal with these situations, and we also protect people from biohazard problems. When you clean up after a body, pathogens, like TB and hepatitis, become airborne. People are scared of AIDS, but AIDS isn't going to kill you. TB and hepatitis are going to get you a lot quicker. AIDS has to be introduced to the body, whereas TB and hepatitis can be breathed in.

To do our job, we wear nonporous suits, rubber boots, gloves, and respirators. The respirators are masks that filter out the impurities, the possible contagions. We have special vacuums and chemical cleaners, but we also use regular mops and brushes, though all our equipment like that is disposable.

The grisliest job we ever had was this industrial accident. This man was sucked into this machine and came out like something blended. There was nothing there that would let you know this had been a human being. I felt terrible for the family. I think for the grieving process, it's important to have a body, to be able to see the person one last time, to have something to hold on to so you can let go.

One thing I'm always asked is how we deal emotionally with trauma scenes. The biggest problem is if you try to block it out. When we're on the job we talk about what we're doing, and we talk about it after the job. My friends and the women in my life are curious and so I tell them what I've seen, and then also you do the normal things that people do to relax from the stress of their work—fun things, family things, weird things. So it's hard, like any work, but it's also an interesting job, because you never know what you're going to be led into. You see people's lives, their homes. It's human to be curious how people live. We get a lot of jobs where the people have OCB—obsessive-compulsive behaviors—where they save everything. They live on top of stuff—newspapers, canned goods, plastic bags. One guy had sixty umbrellas. The families need us to clean this stuff up, throw it out. From one guy's one-bedroom apartment we removed two tractor trailers' worth of stuff. Families are usually embarrassed by this, or they'll be embarrassed because the family member who died had a kinky-sex room, and we have to clean that up, but we don't pass judgment on anyone. We're professional.

Some jobs, of course, are much harder than others. The biggest job we've ever had, and the most emotionally devastating, was the Wendy's restaurant murder scene. Seven people. That job took five days—eight to ten people working midnight to 6 A.M. Wendy's wanted us there during those hours, so that the families wouldn't have to see us cleaning up. They were very considerate of the families, which impressed me. The biggest thing we had to clean up on that job was all the meat that the police had removed from the coolers, which was where the people had been shot; there were hundreds of pounds of contaminated meat. We filled 198 medical waste bags with the meat and had it incinerated. Also, like at most murder scenes, there was fingerprint dust everywhere, and that stuff is hard to remove; so we spent hours getting it off of cash registers, doorjambs, tables, though they may never open that Wendy's again. But it had to be cleaned.

Usually, what bothers us the most on our jobs is not the visual impact of the scenes but the odors. The odors will knock you over, they are so unbelievably strong and putrid. You can be doing this job twenty years and walk into some of these places and still vomit. What the police do at a scene is pour a whole can of coffee into a pot with some water and just let it boil and get the coffee aroma to mask the odors. But for a long time this was a mystery to me—we'd come to a death scene after the police had opened it up and there were always these burnt pots. Didn't matter if you were killed or died naturally, committed suicide, whatever, burnt pots were the common denominator. Then I finally learned, it was all these old-time detectives cooking coffee to help with the odors.

But death itself doesn't bother me—we're all going to die. I'm a realist, if you will. We were called in for this one job and this guy was undiscovered for many months in his own house. He lived alone; people didn't check on him too often. His entire body had broken down, everything had soaked into the wood of the floor; there was nothing left except his bones. It truly is dust to dust. We go right back to where we came from. It makes you want to make every day worth it. I don't care if you're rich or poor, straight or gay, black or white, male or female, whatever, we're all going back to the same place. So what does this tell you? You need to value your time while you're here.

2000

Taking my cure at Yaddo.

MY NEW SOCIETY TESTIMONY: ABLE TO LOVE AGAIN

I was insane and then I was cured by the New Society For Universal Harmony. I'd like to tell you about this cure, but I'll begin with how I went mad.

I loved someone.

She loved me.

Then she stopped loving me. There was an age difference. Not in my favor. I was old. She was young. So she left me. Then she came back. Then she left me. Then she came back. Then . . .

Young people often behave this way, so I'm told. I received the following advice from a friend in the form of a question: "Is the fucking you're getting worth the fucking you're getting?"

Yes.

But then, finally, she didn't come back anymore. I was shattered.

I tried to time how long I could go between thoughts of her. Usually not more than five minutes. I had lost control of my mind. Like something that floats in front of the eye, I saw her all day long and all night long—I dreamt about her repeatedly. Dreamt that she had new lovers, better lovers. In one dream I saw the enormous cock of one of my dream-rivals and screamed out in pain, like I was having a nightmare.

In this utterly damaged state of being, I went up to Yaddo, ostensibly to work on my new novel. But how could I work? Not only were my mind and heart afflicted, but so was my digestion. I had developed irritable bowel syndrome, which is caused primarily by emotional upset. I told a friend at Yaddo my tale of heartbreak and how as a result I needed to be near a toilet at all times, but then concluded, "I still would like to marry the girl. Maybe I can."

My friend, a brilliant novelist, replied, "Go ahead and marry her if you want to wear a diaper the rest of your life."

Then he told me he knew someone who could help me—a Dr. F. A. Mesmer, the founder of the New Society. She had cured him of a severe depression. He gave me her phone number. She was in nearby Athol Springs.

I called Mesmer. She had me outline the problem for her.

"You have a delirious love attachment," she said, and then added, "I can help you." She was intimate with the Yaddo grounds and told me to meet her at the Japanese rock garden at seven the next morning.

"Will this cost anything?" I asked. But she had already hung up. I met Mesmer at the appointed hour. Her eyes were dark liquid holes. She was middle-aged with wiry auburn hair.

"Take your clothes off," she said.

I obeyed her without question. Those eyes. Also, I was willing to try anything.

"Please get into the water."

Yaddo's Japanese garden is an enchanting enclosed glade with an enormous volcanic rock in the center of a pool, which I entered naked. Mesmer handed me a black funnel.

"Put it over your genitals. . . . Stand by the rock. . . . Face me. Listen closely. The human body is a magnet. Love is a result of magnetic harmony between two people. You have a magnetic imbalance. The rock, with its ore, will draw the obsession for the girl out of you; the water, an antimagnetic force, will keep you stabilized and prevent you from getting overcharged."

"Is this dangerous?" What had I gotten myself into?

"The way you are right now is dangerous. You need help. Get in position. Close your eyes. Come out of the water when I tell you."

I followed directions: held the funnel in place, stood in the water. It was cold but magnificent. I don't know how long I was in there. She told me to come out. "You should feel better now," she said. She shook my hand and left.

Over the days that followed, the girl wasn't floating across my eye anymore. I felt sad—she was truly gone. But so was the madness and the IBS. The crazy procedure had actually worked. My mind and colon had been restored! I could feel that I was ready to be magnetically drawn to someone new. I was ready again to love! Mesmer had healed me!

2002

This story was originally written for Bomb *magazine and has since been published in the book* The New Society for Universal Harmony, *which was put out by Granary Books. I think it's only fair to explain that this story is somewhat fictional. Just about everything I wrote was and is true—my ailments, my broken heart, my friend saying that I would need a diaper—but what is false is the character of Dr. Mesmer. Dr. Mesmer is actually an artist named Lenore Malen, who calls herself Dr. F. A. Mesmer as an homage to the famous eighteenth-century hypnotist and radical thinker and possible quack Dr. Franz Mesmer, from whom the word "mesmerize" is derived. Lenore started the New Society for Universal Harmony as some kind of ongoing art project that I have never fully understood. She was at Yaddo when I was there and she asked me to come up with a cure for myself. She didn't ask me if I had a problem of any sort, she just assumed that I did. So I proposed immersing myself in the Japanese rock garden at Yaddo as my cure. She thought this was a great idea and she took the picture you see on page 62. All my dialogue with Dr. Mesmer is made up, as is the advice from my friend to contact Dr. Mesmer. What's really interesting—and not made up—was that after standing naked in the rock garden I actually did feel better. I had come up with a cure that worked!*

The-nearly-pain-free-breakup (tha-nir'le-pan-fre-brak-up), n. Something that happens between two people who have been romantically involved but for a number of reasons—usually idiotic but not always—can no longer be together. So for years—well, millennia—there was no way of getting around it: When a love affair came to an end it hurt. It hurt very badly. It was number five on the pain-chart after (1) death of a loved one; (2) disease or physical injury; (3) false imprisonment for a crime you didn't commit; and (4) torture or attack by a malevolent person. Since numbers three and four weren't—thank God—that typical for most people, heartbreak was a real problem. Then, in 2016, Breakup Clinics, affiliated with Curves exercise studios, began to pop up all over the country. These clinics offered classes in guided meditation, prayer, and self-massage. Also, you could lie for as long as you liked on a super-cozy "healing" bed with a real nice comforter to hide under, and, if you liked, an adult pacifier was put in your mouth. Meanwhile self-esteem mantras were pumped into your head via pillow-sized headphones. One of the biggest breakthroughs in breakup healing, discovered by the founder of the clinics, Susan Pearlstein, was that the old cop-out "It's not you, it's me" was actually true. It was proved that all breakups had nothing to do with your self-worth; it had to do with something going on in the other person. This was very helpful, since a great deal of the pain involved in breakups has to do with a feeling of rejection. In addition, there is, naturally, a terrible sense of loss. Severe loneliness also enters into it—the knowledge that all human beings are essentially alone, trapped inside their own minds and behind the masks of their faces. But the clinics make this all quite manageable and restore us to our usual blithe, distracted, mildly sad but functional selves. Also, the clinics have turned out to be great places to meet newly single people. Granted everyone is on the rebound, but this was another Great Truth discovered by Ms. Pearlstein: We're all perpetually on the rebound. This, it was discovered, has to do with the spinning of the earth and the ubiquity of the spiral in all forms of life. So it came to be that a lot of people eventually crawled into the healing beds together and new romances were sparked, restarting the perpetual cycle of love and pain, love and pain, love and pain.

SELF-SENTENCED:
MY LIFE AS A WRITER
THE LAST FEW YEARS

I: My Big Artistic Breakthrough

For a year, circa 1995, I was living in New Jersey with my parents due to financial problems—I was broke—but then I was awarded a grant for a few thousand dollars. With this money and the small income I received from teaching composition at a business college, I was able to move back to New York, where I rented a cheap room from a dear friend of mine, a beautiful woman, an artist. We had once briefly been quasi-lovers during one of my residencies at Yaddo, but we never had sexual intercourse—we realized we were more like brother and sister than boyfriend and girlfriend—and so we were ideal roommates. If we had made love, living together probably wouldn't have worked. You know how it is.

Anyway, the day I moved in was the first time I was ever in her apartment (I took my room sight unseen; one can only live with one's parents for so long) and I was shocked to observe that on her bookshelf were numerous novels by my hero—I'm not ashamed to admit it—Charles Bukowski. I didn't think women read him. I naively assumed they all hated him because of the way he wrote about screwing women and slapping women and everything else he did to them. I said to my friend, "I can't believe you read Bukowski."

"I love Bukowski," she said. "I only wish I had gone to L.A. and fucked him before he died."

Thunderclap!

Burning bush!

Wet bush!

$E=mc^2$!

This was my big artistic breakthrough! Kind of like when Jonathan Franzen read Paula Fox's *Desperate Characters* and realized what a novel could do. I'm referring to his famous *Harper's* article, which I've actually read, with some skimming, though I haven't read *The Corrections*—it's much too long and expensive (I can't afford hardcovers), but it looks very good. In the *Harper's* piece, Jonathan recalls how after reading Fox's novel, he felt less alone in the world and he wanted to write a book that made others feel less alone. I have the same noble goal for my writing, but with a selfish caveat: One of the people I'd like to see feeling less lonely is me. That's where my artistic breakthrough comes in.

You see, Bukowski often wrote about young women wanting to sleep with him (or his fictional stand-in, Henry

Chinaski) because of his stories and poems, and I had always thought he was bullshitting. Bukowski was the self-described ugliest man of all time—photographs of his acne-scarred face make you realize he wasn't exaggerating—and I figured he got off on fantasizing about screwing lots of female fans and creating an alternative life for himself in his books. But with my friend's statement, I realized that Bukowski was telling the truth. If she wanted to go to L.A. and sleep with him, so must have hundreds of others.

I now had the key to all I desired. I was thirty-one years old and had learned something very important about writing and the female psyche: If I put in my stories my profound appreciation of women's rear ends, legs, breasts—hell, the whole body!—and my desire to lick women everywhere and mount them from behind, then women would gobble this stuff up and I'd get laid just like Bukowski. We men have to learn this Golden Rule over and over: Women want to be wanted and they love sex.

II. Busy Destroying a Name for Myself

I unfortunately couldn't put my Bukowski plan into action right away. I was working on my second novel, *The Extra Man*, and with the writing of that book I was busy exorcising homoerotic and transvestite issues, which, come to think of it, I had tried to exorcise in my first novel, *I Pass Like Night*. I must be the gayest straight writer in America.

Well, I exorcised things so well in *The Extra Man* that my own publisher sent me cross-dressing books as presents for several years. I am not a transvestite!

But with my *New York Press* column, which I started in 1997, I had the chance to redeem my reputation, or, rather, create a better false one. Everyone thought I was gay or a cross-dresser, and I had to undo this. So I created a persona designed, like Bukowski's, to attract women, and the system, I must admit, worked pretty well. The letters, photographs, and e-mails started coming in. Women, mostly young girls, wanted to meet me!

I should tell you that I've had other role models besides Bukowski, all of them equally alcoholic and self-destructive. As a young boy I used to pretend I was certain baseball or basketball stars, and then in high school I switched to writers. First I wanted to be Hunter Thompson, but then I quickly dropped him for Jack Kerouac. He was so handsome. I used to love to look at pictures of him, and sometimes I still do, like looking at photos of a girl I once adored. Then in college, there was Hemingway and Fitzgerald, both of whom gave me lots of excuses to drink.

In my late twenties, I tried to be Thomas Mann, but that was too much work. In my mid-thirties, I was briefly Graham Greene, when I wasn't being Bukowski. Nowadays I don't know who I am. I need a new role model. I may try to be P. G. Wodehouse, but he was awfully prolific.

Anyway, in 2000, I published two years' worth of my Bukowskiesque *Press* stuff in a book called *What's Not to Love?: The Adventures of a Mildly Perverted Young Writer*. Now the thing is if you tell the world you're perverted they believe you, just as Dave Eggers told the world he's a Genius and Franzen told the world he's a Great American Novelist and everybody believed those two and rightly so. But I really screwed up.

Geniuses and Great American Novelists sell a hell of a lot more books than Perverts. I should sue myself for libel. Just the other day, I said to a friend of mine, "I've made a mess of my life." And he said, "No you haven't, you've made a career of your life."

Girls may want to meet me, but no one actually takes my writing seriously. My whole oeuvre has become one big dysfunctional personal ad. My therapist, with whom I do phone sessions at highly discounted rates, said to me recently, "Your life is an open book, warts and all."

"Quite literally," I said, and reminded him that I had written extensively about my traumatic experience in 1984 with a venereal wart. He apologized, worried that he had wounded me, and I told him he hadn't, though his sentence with two metaphors—"open book, warts and all"—might have wounded a less forgiving writer than myself.

This open-book thing, I have to tell you, can really backfire. I dated this one girl who hadn't read my work—an anomaly—and before the second date she had heard from five different sources that I was a homosexual, a womanizer, a cross-dresser, a purveyor of prostitutes, and a fancier of transsexuals. Gossip stings, especially when you're the source of it. I couldn't believe people were reading my work so closely. Luckily, the information the girl received was so contradictory (no person could be all those things, she reasoned; but little did she know!) that she didn't dump me and we actually fell in love.

Then she read the books and the shit hit the fan, literally and metaphorically. She didn't like all the sex and she absolutely loathed the scatological aspect of my art.

"But sex scenes and bathroom jokes are my bread and butter," I pleaded.

But there was a look in her eye and so I started writing a novel where people don't go to the bathroom and don't have sex and this pleased her, and I consoled myself with the thought that all artists have worked with censorship. But then recently she left me—well, a year ago; I tend to hold on to these things—and now I'm brokenhearted and halfway through a completely clean book. Well, there's hope, I guess. In the second half of the book, I'm going to have a sex scene and at least one scatological reference. I may even, as an act of spite, combine the two. I think it was Shakespeare who said: "To thine own self be true."

I shouldn't complain, since this is the bed I've made, but lately the young girls have been driving me crazy. One night four coeds were Instant Messaging me at the same time. I was typing furiously. My laptop was like some kind of erotic switch-board. Most of these college girls have orgasm problems and after reading *What's Not to Love?* they come to me as if I'm some kind of guru. Taking a professorial tone, I give all of them the same assignment: Read Lonnie Barbach's tome on female mas-turbation, *For Yourself,* do the exercises she recommends, and then e-mail me a book report on the experience.

I do hope I'm not coming across as too one-dimensional. Besides girls, there are other important people in my life. For example, there's my wonderful sixteen-year-old son, who has read only one of my essays. But from that one piece he fig-ured everything out; he said, "I know what you do: You make a living making fun of yourself."

And then, of course, there's my mother and father. I'm often asked: "How do your parents deal with your books?" Well, when my father read a chapter from an early draft of my first novel, he said, "I'm never speaking to you again." So I didn't show either parent anything more of that book for some time, but then before publication, I went with my mother and father to a family counselor and told them what was true and what was not true, and ever since that session they've been heroically accepting of me. In fact, I sometimes perform as a stand-up comedian and I tell stories about smoking crack and consorting with transsexuals, and my mother and father sit in the back of the nightclub laughing happily. I guess my parents know that life is short and they might as well get a kick out of things. I also think they're not really listening to me.

III. The Brothers Jonathan

So I've destroyed my name with the things I've written, and what's made it worse is that there are so many talented young writers named Jonathan, with whom by comparison I suffer terribly, furthering the damage I've already done to myself. There's Franzen, Lethem, Dee, a Brit named Coe, and this new young writer, Safran Foer, who went to my alma mater, Princeton, and who recently sold his much-anticipated first novel for several hundred thousand dollars, which I read about in *Entertainment Weekly*.

I have to say that with all these Jonathans running around, it's like we're *The Brothers Karamazov*, and I see myself as the sickly, subnormal brother who is always wandering off into the black Russian forest and is found screwing sap holes in trees. He's then brought back to the family and the father whips him.

IV. The Erections

After Cervantes published *Don Quixote*, somebody wrote a sequel and published it under the name Cervantes, hoping to make some money. This, naturally, infuriated Cervantes and so he penned the true sequel to his book, and poor Don Quixote, in book two, as he went on further adventures, had to deal with the very postmodern fact that there were two histories about him, one false and one real, kind of like my life. I've put too many versions out there. I'm like Stalin but with my own history. I don't know what the truth is anymore. What has really happened? I should write myself a happy ending.

I think my next career move will be to change my name to Franzen—which shouldn't be too hard, since it's only the surname that I'll have to change—and write, like the Cervantes impostor, a sequel to *The Corrections* called *The Erections*. I'll self-publish the thing and make a few thousand bucks before anyone catches on. Only problem is Franzen will then get all the girls who are excited by *The Erections*. Well, that's all right. I may be perverted, but I'm not ungenerous.

2002

I LOVE YOU MORE
THAN YOU KNOW

I try to call my great-aunt Doris every day. She's ninety and lives alone. I love her desperately and as she gets older—especially of late, as she becomes more feeble—my love seems to be picking up velocity, overwhelming me almost, tinged as it is with panic: I'm so afraid of losing her.

I usually call her around six o'clock and when she picks up the phone, she always says, "Hellooooo," drawing out the *o*'s to sound like a society lady, but when she's not feeling well the *o*'s aren't so drawn out, so I like it when her affectation is present. Daily, we have just about the same conversation.

"Do you need any money?" she says. "Don't be ashamed to tell me. Aunt Doris is here to help you." Sometimes she speaks of herself in the third person, like a professional athlete.

"I don't need any money," I say, "but thank you."

"Have you had your dinner yet?"

"No, I'm going out."

"Treat yourself to a steak. You're not a vegetarian anymore, are you?"

"No, not a vegetarian."

"That's smart. A steak is good for you. Wear a hat when you go out."

My period of vegetarianism about ten years ago still haunts her, and she's been telling me to wear a hat for over thirty years.

"Well, I'll talk to you tomorrow," I say. "I love you."

"I love you more than that," she says.

*   *   *

My great-aunt was raised in Saratoga Springs, New York, one of six children, including my grandmother Nancy, who died several years ago. When my great-aunt was ten her mother died, and she and Nancy had to take care of their father, the house, and the boys (three brothers), as well as the infant son of their sister Anna, who had died in childbirth.

When she was fifteen my great-aunt started working as a manicurist in a beauty shop, Fresham's, where she attended to the wealthy ladies who came to Saratoga for the racing season, and this was to be her lifelong profession.

In the thirties, she'd follow the wealthy set—always working at a different Fresham's—by the seasons: Saratoga in August, New York City in the fall, Miami Beach in the winter, and resorts along the eastern seaboard in the spring. By the forties, she was in New York full-time working in the salon at Saks Fifth Avenue. She had a brief marriage during the war years, followed by a ten-year marriage in the fifties, and then in the sixties she was single again and worked for many years in the barbershop at the Harmonie, a private men's club off Park Avenue. In my family, she was legendary for being a wild, great beauty: a tiny, stunning, voluptuous redhead who had many lovers; a sort of Jewish Holly Golightly.

She wasn't able to have children and so my mother, her sister's daughter, was like a child to her and I, later, was like a grandchild, and clearly her favorite. All throughout my childhood, she'd come to New Jersey to visit us for weekends. I loved to meet her with my mother at the little station—she'd descend out of the bus in her colorful dresses and heels, and kiss me a thousand times, but I didn't mind.

When she was in her mid-seventies, my great-aunt lost a breast to cancer, and for the last twenty years she has lived in Queens in her tiny studio apartment. Her couch is her bed, the place is cluttered with antiques but kept neat, and there are many paintings on the walls. My favorites are these small watercolors done by a French lover of hers, whom she met in Paris in 1947. All of them feature a tiny redheaded woman with an hourglass figure—you see her sitting in a cafe, standing on a bridge over the Seine, kissing a lover on a park bench under a night sky.

* * *

Two weeks ago, I went to see my great-aunt on a Sunday, as is our habit. I make it out there about twice a month. When I can't make it, she always says to me, "If I can't see you, we still have our telephone romance."

Right in her subway stop is a little florist, and I picked up some irises. She smiled so happily when she saw me. I hugged her to my chest—she's very small—and stroked her hair, which is no longer flame red but has faded to a pretty strawberry blonde.

Our routine is to have lunch and then play gin rummy, but before playing cards I told her I wanted to talk to her about her life, that I was going to write an article about her for *Vogue*[5] magazine, which impressed her. Most of the magazines I've written for she hasn't heard of. We sat on her couch.

"You already know everything," she said.

"I want to make sure I've got the stories right."

"What should I tell you then?"

"Just some memories. What do you remember from Saratoga?"

"From Saratoga . . . I remember when Mother died. I was ten years old and Nancy was eleven. I knew that a person wore black. So we went to the dime store and bought black dye and put our kerchiefs and gloves in the dye, and when I finished my hands were black—couldn't get that off. Washed. Scoured. For two weeks I walked around with black hands."

Eighty years later, my great-aunt still sometimes cries about this—her mother's early death shaped her whole life, took away her childhood.

---

[5] *Vogue* was going to run this essay, but then it was pushed to a later issue, and then ultimately the magazine ended up not using it and it was published by www.mrbellersneighborhood.com.

"What do you remember from working in Saratoga?" I asked.

"Let me get my thoughts. . . . How old was I? Sixteen. Working at the Grand Union Hotel. A woman came in for a manicure. She was looking for prostitutes, but I didn't know that. This was in the thirties. She says, 'When you come to New York call me.' I was supposed to go to New York to work and wait until the season started in Miami Beach. There—"

"In Miami?"

"Don't say Miami. Miami Beach. There I had the experience of manicuring the wife of the writer Damon Runyon. She was a bitch. After I put four coats of polish on her, she rubbed it off. Said she wanted to see if redheads had a temper. Can you imagine? I also took care of Mrs. Jimmy Walker there, the wife of the mayor of New York."

"What happened to the woman who was looking for the prostitutes?"

"The madam? I called her when I got to New York."

"What happened? You didn't work for her, did you?" This would have been new information. The family didn't know about this!

"She told me she wanted me to be a prostitute, and that was the end of that, naturally. I said, 'You've got the wrong girl.'"

"Really?"

"Of course."

"In the thirties is when you had the abortion?" I asked. It may sound like I was being rude, but my great-aunt and I have talked about everything for years.

"Yes, that was the thirties. When I had that I went to the drugstore. 'Al,' I said to him. 'My best girl friend is pregnant. I have to help her.' So he gave me the name of a doctor, also in Brooklyn. I got an appointment, a private house. This wasn't legit. Got me on a table—not even an aspirin. Spread my legs. Not even an aspirin! Took an instrument; hurt like hell. Wonder I didn't die from the pain. Lasted ten minutes. He says, 'You stay here until I tell you to go home.' He comes back a few minutes later, I'm still bleeding, says I should go home. I go home and I tell Nancy it's my period. It was my secret. I didn't tell anyone. Two days later I stopped bleeding. And then it became a memory."

"Did that keep you from having children?"

"More or less, I think so. . . . Let me get my papers, there are things in there that'll be good for an article."

She went to a drawer and removed an envelope stuffed with letters and clippings—obituaries of her Harmonie clients, most of whom were well-to-do businessmen.

She began reading the obituaries, and she came across one, on a yellowed piece of newspaper, and kissed it. "This one I loved," she said. "Had a real crush on him. We had an affair. He was so sweet. He cared for me. What people I had in my life. Good people."

"When did you have an affair with him?"

"I don't know. Before he died! I can't remember everything."

She found another obit. "This one was crazy about me. Those were good days. I had my apartment on Fifteenth Street. I had my little dog. He didn't like the dog."

"Did you have an affair?"

"Not really. He just liked to be near me. He wasn't interested in sex. Neither was I. His car would drop him off at my house. He'd just sit on the couch. Liked to be near me."

"How many lovers do you think you had in your life?"

"What's your idea of a lover?"

"Someone you had sex with."

"I don't know. I can't figure that out. I was very active in sex. I was sexy."

"Make a guess."

"Six."

"That's it? Your whole life?"

"You want to add two, add two. I didn't screw around with everybody. These were men who stayed. But I didn't play it right. I screwed my life up."

"How so?"

"I had offers to live on Fifth Avenue. I had wonderful chances. I was too . . . not pious . . . too righteous. I always knew the difference between good and bad and I always chose good. I should have relaxed and done a little bad. I should have stuck with one good man and not cared if he had a wife. Now look at me."

"Are you saying a man would have taken care of you?"

"Sure. Why would I be a mistress to him if he didn't give me a car, an apartment. I wouldn't have to live like this on a couch. These were wealthy men. Not salesmen. The mistress sometimes gets more than the wife. Don't you know that?"

We looked at the clippings for a while longer. "I wish I knew some of the people I used to know," she said, and put everything back in the envelope.

We were quiet, and then she said, "What's happening with you, lover-boy? You pop out girlfriends like pizza pies."

"I'm still hung up on this one girl," I said. "She doesn't want to be with me. Did you ever have that, where you think about someone all the time?"

"Worse. The people are dead—they never come back. But time heals, and in that time you just run away from it, and running away means you get involved with someone else quick. . . . Where is this girl?"

"Out of the country. Has a new boyfriend."

"So let him enjoy her. It's past tense. It's gone. If you don't want to get over it, it will stay with you, that's for sure."

"Should I try to get her back?"

"A lot of fish in the ocean, brother. Lots of fish."

"But how come I can't stop thinking about her?"

"Like me with all the people in here"—she squeezed the envelope—"but you have to go on without thinking. If you can't work up a veneer around your heart you'll wind up going to a psychiatrist and throwing your money away. . . . Know what makes a person strong? You have to take failure. Another person had to experience what I had to experience, they'd go on the booze and stay on the booze until they dropped dead. You don't see me doing that. If I had to take my life serious, I'd be up shit's creek."

"I wish I could get over this girl."

"You pine for her. Bullshit. I wouldn't give her a minute of my time. She doesn't think of you; it's a one-sided affair. What's good is that you don't need her. You're intelligent, re-spectable home, good-looking, you're not out of prison—you don't need her. Choose a good woman, not a cold tomato. Forget her."

"Of course I haven't been to prison!"

"That's because you're from a good family."

"Anyway, didn't you ever pine for someone?"

"No, not me. I want respect. If I don't get respect, they can go fly a kite. . . . Where'd you get this haircut?"

"My neighborhood, why?"

"I don't like it. It's not tapered in the back. Looks like a wig."

That cracked me up, so we stopped talking about love and went and played cards. As usual, she won. Then she walked me out to the elevator. I hugged her while we waited for it. "I worry about you," I said.

"Don't worry about Aunt Doris. I'm a survivor. It's my job to worry about you."

"All right," I said, consoled. The elevator came. I got in and held the door. "I love you," I said.

"I love you more than you know," she said, and she leaned in and kissed me good-bye.

2002

EVERYBODY DIES
IN MEMPHIS

About two hours after the Tyson-Lewis fight, after the arena had cleared out, after the final press conference, after twenty thousand people had collectively shot some kind of cathartic wad of soul-semen and soul-pussy-juice, I found an exit and walked alone across a large, desolate parking lot and up a steep grass embankment. As usual I had fucked up. This was no way to leave the Pyramid arena. To get back to the world, which was a dangerous dark road underneath a highway, I had to climb a high metal fence. I could have turned back, found a proper exit, but, naturally, I didn't. I was too lazy to retrace my steps, but not too lazy to climb a fence. In other words, I'm an idiot.

So at the top of the fifteen-foot-high fence, as I swung my leg over, my pants, right in the crotch area, got caught in the sharp, rusted wire, which wasn't razor wire, but was just as effective.

Oh, no, Ames, I said to myself, *don't rip up your cock, not at one A.M. in Memphis.*

I couldn't get leverage to unhook my crotch, because I couldn't put my hands down on the wire to push off—it would have sliced me up immediately. My fists were in the last safe rung of fencing, and my feet were in holes on either side.

So I was stuck up there, legs straddled, dick near-pierced, feet starting to slip, and a subnormal man in thick glasses and a dirty baseball cap came limping along, carrying a stack of just printed "Limited Editions" of the local paper, with the headline, *Lewis KO's Tyson in 8.* He was some kind of southern homeless man, face contorted and weird from retardation, but the eyes behind the thick glasses were kind and gentle—the disposition of all the Memphians I had met.

"What are you doing on that fence? Are you lost?" he asked.

Lost? "I'm stuck," I said, and looked at him in the silvery light cast by the parking lot below.

"Did you go to the fight?" he asked.

"Yes."

"I'm going to sell these papers!" he said, wanting praise and affirmation from me in his childlike, retarded way. He was still searching, as most of us are, retarded or not, for a father to pat him on the back. He looked to be about fifty.

"That's good," I said, and my feet slipped some more. I could feel the loser in me wanting to just let go, give up, get a tetanus gash in my penis or scrotum, and then fall to the ground and break a wrist. But there was the possibility of the cock getting ripped off and me falling to the ground without it, and even the loser in me didn't want to see my penis left behind on some rusty wire.

So there I was on the precipice of castrating injury, and not too far away, Denzel Washington was probably doing lines of coke, and the scores of NBA stars who had come to the fight were probably having their impossibly long dicks sucked by one of the thousands of whores who had descended on Memphis, and David Remnick, *The New Yorker* editor, who had come as the thinking man's observer of the fight, was probably having a nice late dinner and talking to someone intelligent, before getting his own dick sucked by one of the thousands of whores. Wait a second, I take that back. I spoke to Remnick briefly. He seemed classy. So he probably wouldn't get his dick sucked, which is my way of saying: I hope I get published in *The New Yorker* someday, Mr. Remnick, should you happen to read this.

Anyway, back to the fence. The subnormal man said, "You want to buy one of my papers?"

"I've got to get down first," I shouted at him.

And then somehow, I did it. I got my leverage toe in a hole, pushed off, the crotch unsnagged, and I shakily scaled down the other side. I bought a paper from the man for two dollars, and he staggered away underneath the highway into oblivion, heading in the direction of the beautiful brown Mississippi, which bisects our country like the world's largest septic line. Why the subnormal was going in that direction, away from town where he could sell his papers, I have no idea.

So I, the less retarded of the two of us, though not by much, crossed the road, got out from underneath the highway, and went into the first bar I came across, even though I don't drink anymore. But I was thirsty from my exertions and craved a club soda. The bar was simply a door in the back of a building. There was nothing else around. I was in some urban dead zone next to the highway. Over the door was a sign that said *Discretions* and there was a neon beer bottle in a window. I sensed something perverted about the place; I have a good nose for these things. I went in and walked down a hall. At the end of the hall, a little shiny-faced fellow sat on a stool.

"Five-dollar cover," he said.

I wasn't sure I wanted to pay five bucks to get into what looked like a dive just to order a club soda, and the shiny fellow saw me hesitate. "Normally it's forty," he said, to lure me, going into his sales pitch, "but because of the fight, we're offering a discount, five dollars, and with that you can become a member of Discretions. You know this is a swingers' club, right?"

"No, I didn't know," I said. "What do you mean by a swingers' club?"

So I was right—the place was perverted. But I was unsure if "swinger" meant the same thing in Memphis as it did in New York. Swingers' clubs in New York, like Plato's Retreat, have long since expired. Could they possibly still be alive in Tennessee? Then again, my whole experience for three days in Memphis had left me feeling like I had traveled back in time, as if Elvis's death had permanently frozen the city in the year 1977. So I shouldn't have been shocked to come upon a swingers' club.

"It's a bar for couples to meet, and singles, too," the little man on the stool said. "Alternative lifestyles."

So, sure enough, the definition was the same in Memphis as in New York, and while not a swinger, I could definitely fall under the heading of "alternative," so I paid my five dollars and went into the swingers' club to swing my dick, to celebrate its not having been severed on that terrible fence.

Well, that was the start of my last night in Tennessee, and I promise I'll return the story to Discretions, to that lovely club, but I'd like to go back to the very beginning of my trip to Memphis, a journey I had taken so I could see a fight, see something violent and terrible—I hoped—and then to be able to say, "*I* was there."

Therefore, it was an ego trip, which is always the worst kind of trip to take. It's that old hubris problem. The gods don't like ego; you show too much of it and they stick you on fences and threaten to remove your genitals, metaphorically or otherwise. But enough of that fence, and as I said, let me go back to the beginning, when I first came to Memphis, to this town where Mike Tyson was beaten to a bloody pulp, where Elvis lived and died, where Martin Luther King Jr. was shot dead, where the blues were born, and where so much of lurid America seems to have come down the Mississippi and washed up on the banks.

Thursday, June 6, 11 A.M.

I take a taxi from the airport and go directly to the Cook Convention Center to pick up my credentials and attend the weigh-ins of the fighters—Lewis at noon, Tyson at three. I plan to check into my sleazy hotel later.

The lobby of the convention center is loaded with cops in riot gear. I give my name and passport and get some kind of wristband. Then a cop frisks me and waves his bomb-detector wand in my armpits and up my ass. No bombs there, except for my sporadic explosive episodes of irritable bowel syndrome with which I destroy toilets and soil the back of my shirttails wherever I go.

After being frisked, I go to a room where I get my temporary credentials and have my picture taken for my permanent credentials, which I'll get the next day. Then I head up some stairs to the Media Center, where I pick up all sorts of folders and press releases. There are dozens of journalists typing at their laptops, and radio guys, with miniature broadcast stations, are talking into microphones. Mounted TVs blast ESPN. I'm in sports-journalist heaven and feel kind of giddy. I can't believe I've pulled this off: press credentials for the Tyson-Lewis fight! A weirdo writer like me. But, also, secretly, I'm a mad, closet sports fan. I see Remnick. I see recently deposed *Post* columnist Wallace Matthews. I'm with the big boys.

I go up another flight of stairs to an enormous hangarlike space, capable of holding rock concerts, political rallies. There are two hundred chairs set up and a stage with a white scale that looks like a cross.

I grab a seat right in the front row. I look around— Leroy Neiman, the famous fight painter, is at the other end of my row. He's drawing a picture of the scale. He has a Dali mustache and is wearing elaborate white and black shoes. An old man with white hair, leaning on a cane, stands next to him.

Journalists from all over the world are filling up the chairs. Behind us is another stage with dozens of high-powered cameras with black cannonlike lenses pointing at the scale. So much attention for two men fighting. We've got whole countries fighting. There are huge problems to solve. But I've long since accepted that the world is sick, imbalanced, and lunatic. So while we live with the constant specter of terror, while chunks of polar ice caps are breaking off, while the Mideast self-immolates, I and thousands of others are gathered in Memphis to see two black men attack one another.

There's a British photographer sitting next to me, and I ask him, "Excuse me, but do you know who the guy with the white hair and the cane is?"

"That's Buddie Schulberg," says the Brit.

Schulberg wrote *On the Waterfront.* He penned the line "I coulda been a contender." No wonder he's at the fight. "I'm going to try to talk to him and Neiman," I say to the photog.

"Don't bother with Neiman. He's just here to sell paintings. A prostitute."

Suddenly, Neiman does look a little whorish to me. That mustache. Those shoes. I'm very impressionable. I go over to Schulberg. I hear him say to another reporter, "It could be Shakespearean."

The reporter leaves. "Mr. Schulberg, excuse me," I say, "but did I hear you say you thought the fight could be Shakespearean?"

"I think something out of Shakespeare could happen to Tyson," he says. "There's this violence inside him. I worry that something terrible will happen and he'll come to a terrible end." Schulberg speaks in the sweet, halting tones of an older man.

"Do you think something bad could happen in this fight?"

"I don't know," he says.

"Who do you think is going to win?"

"It's a tough fight to call. Such a mental game. Lewis has to take the fight away from Tyson right away, like Holyfield did. But Tyson doesn't have the jab he used to. He might be naked in there."

I can't think of any more boxing questions, so I say, "I read once about your cross-country trip with F. Scott Fitzgerald."

"Yes, I wrote about that in *The Disenchanted*."

"The two of you got drunk on a plane and then went to the Winter Carnival at Dartmouth, right?"

"Yes. Scott started out sober. But my father ordered Mums champagne for the flight, and nobody warned me about Scott's problem. Once he started with the champagne that was it."

"What was Fitzgerald like?"

"He was immensely appealing, awfully likable. He was interested in you, would really listen. He was interested in *people*."

I love hearing about Fitzgerald, but then two policemen on motorcycles come roaring into the hangar, followed by three police cars and three white SUVs. Lewis has arrived! Mr. Schulberg and I stop speaking. Lewis emerges from his car—tall, sunglasses, sweat suit, a Rastafarian hat. He's a physically beautiful human being and I wonder if I'm watching a dead man walking. Lewis is the superior boxer, but

Tyson has a lethal punch. If he can land it maybe Lewis dies. That's why we're all here.

Lewis gets on the stage; he's surrounded by his "team," his bodyguards—about twenty large black men in powder-blue sweat suits. SWAT team cops with guns and clubs and biceps line the front of the stage. Lewis's trainer, Emanuelle Steward, undresses Lewis—helps him remove his pants. I once had an amateur fight and my trainer would be intimate like that with me—taking off my clothes, rubbing me down. Trainers are like mothers; they're kind to you, sweet, gentle.

Lewis steps onto the scale, wearing just a pair of gray briefs. He's six-foot-five and powerfully built; his hands and arms are enormous; his hair is in braids. I'm not gay, I'm more straight than gay, though I've been known to be crooked, and so I notice the prodigious outline of Lewis's drooping trunklike cock. How embarrassing for him. Or rather how embarrassing for all us normal-to-underendowed men. Lewis raises his arms in the traditional boxer's pose. White stuff is in his armpits. Cameras flash repeatedly. The announcer calls out, "Two hundred and forty-nine pounds and a quarter."

Lewis steps off the scale. One of his handlers helps him to dress.

1 P.M.

After a free lunch provided for the media—pulled pork, cole-slaw, and beans—I leave the convention center to get some fresh air. At the front of the center, there are six Tyson protestors—four lesbians and two gay men. They're holding signs that say, *Tyson Opposes Homophobia, Thanks Mike!* and

Thanks Mike for Saying Gay Is OK! I figure their signs are a joke, ironic. I approach one of the lesbians, an overweight girl with nose piercings and very pretty blue eyes.

"Your sign is a joke, right?" I say.

"Oh, no. Mike hugged that fellow over there," she says, pointing to a swishy little blond fellow, "and said—these are his exact words—'I oppose all antigay discrimination.' Everyone is quick to judge him, to give him bad press, so it's important to give him good press when he does something appropriate."

I go to the next lesbian, a waifish girl, cute, also with nose piercings. I'd like to ask her for a date.

"What group are you guys all with?" I ask.

"Some of us are Memphis Area Gay Youth, but also Equality of Tennessee, and that man"—she points to a skinny, scary Edgar Allan Poe–type—"is with Outrage, an organization in London. We just want to support Mike for making a step in the direction of tolerance."

"Have you heard any rumors that Mike Tyson might be bisexual?" I ask. I'm dying to imply that his prison time may account for his pro-gay sentiments, but I don't want to be rude.

The girl hesitates. Then she says, "Well, from past comments it seems like he *is* very caught up with anal sex. Some people say he's repressed."

I go over to the little blond boy who created this whole stir.

"How did Tyson come to hug you?" I ask.

"Well, we were protesting at his training camp, trying to raise consciousness about homophobia in sports, and he came out of his car and just hugged me and he said, 'I oppose all—'"

"I know," I say. "So what was it like to be hugged by him?"

This guy is clearly jazzed by the encounter. He's all lit up from within, kind of like Cinderella before midnight. TV cameras are on him, pictures are being snapped.

"I was shocked," he says. "But I wasn't scared. I had to smile and hug him back—being an activist, you know."

"Are you going to root for him to win?" I ask, which is my polite way of saying, *Are you in love with him now that he's held you?*

"I'm opposed to boxing," he says. "I'm a nonviolent person. I just hope neither gets hurt. We're here to raise consciousness. Using antigay words in sports, you know, like 'homo,' 'fag'"—he whispers "homo" and "fag"—"are just as bad as racist words, like the N word."

"Come on, you're not going to root for him? He hugged you!"

"Well, I hope he doesn't get hurt."

What the hell, he's a sweet kid, and I leave him to be pounced on by ten other eager journalists. It's his big day. Belle of the ball.

3 P.M.

Three motorcycle cops, four police cars, and five SUVs—Tyson's entrance is more grand than Lewis's. He comes onto the stage and strips himself. His bodyguards, unlike Lewis's, are ragtag, no uniformity of outfit. Tyson's smiling, chewing gum. He throws some punches. He looks to be in good shape. He has enormous pectoral breasts, which must further endear him to the gay community. He jumps onto the scale. He's wearing shorts; you can't tell if his cock is as big as Lewis's. He weighs in at 234.

I had been looking forward to this moment of seeing Tyson in person. But it's a letdown. I read some article recently—don't remember where—which said that scientists have proven that Americans think they have more friends than they actually have because they watch so much TV. Our primitive brains, still using Stone Age operating systems, are designed to think that a face we see often is a friendly face, so if we watch a lot of TV we come to think that these *faces,* these TV people, these celebrities, are our friends. And that's what I experience when I see Tyson. My brain tells me that I know him already, that he's an old pal. So what's the big deal? Hence, the letdown. So I think that maybe if I could touch him or smell him or be hit by him that would be exciting. But there's no chance I'll get close enough.

A woman journalist behind me, looking at Tyson on the scale, says in a southern drawl, "He's quite a specimen." There's a sexy hint of desire in her voice. I think of Sylvia Plath's line, "Every woman adores a Fascist, / The boot in the face, the brute. . . ."

3:40 P.M.

Press conference with Tyson's handlers. Stacy Mitchell, one of his longtime trainers, is asked, "Why do you think there's such a fascination with Mike Tyson in this country?"

"Not just this country," Mitchell says. "All over the world. People in England slept outside his hotel. When he was on the street they followed him; he had to run to a police station. Can you imagine Mike Tyson running to the *poh-leece*? And here in America we're a violent race of people. We like to be entertained with violence. People like hockey. People like Mike Tyson. He can break jaws, fracture skulls, break bones. You'll see, the South is going to rise again. Mike Tyson is going to rise it. I like Memphis. Good catfish. Collard greens. Stars are here. Mike Tyson is putting Memphis on the map. Feeding people in Tennessee."

7 P.M.

After checking into my hotel on the outskirts, I come back to downtown Memphis and attend a minor-league baseball game. I've been given free tickets because I'm a member of the media, and I get a free meal: hot dogs, beans, coleslaw. The local team is the Redbirds, a Triple-A affiliate of the St. Louis Cardinals.

The stadium is beautiful, brand-new: a cross between Camden Yards and Fenway Park. The game is enjoyable. I'm really in America. A balmy night. Baseball. Families. Children. Toxic food. Beer.

John Rocker, who derailed his career with a terrible racist interview in *Sports Illustrated,* comes in to pitch for the other team, the Redhawks, affiliate of the Texas Rangers. He's been demoted to the minors. He's bigger than the other players, very muscular, his legs like a ballet dancer's. He throws the ball extremely hard—98 mph. But he gets hit and is visibly frustrated. The guy is all will and force. Destined to fail.

The Redbirds have glorious young cheerleaders, a couple of white girls and a couple of black girls. They wear red miniskirts and red bra tops. They stand on the Redbirds dugout and incite the crowd, waving their suggestive pompoms, like they've pulled out a handful of hair from their beautiful young muffs.

9:30 P.M.

I'm on Beale Street, four blocks of blues clubs, neon signs, blaring music, street musicians, Gang Unit police, thousands of people, beer flowing. It's the only street that is alive in Memphis. Everything else is empty 1970s storefronts—abandoned, forgotten.

I don't go into any of the clubs; they're too crowded and there's plenty of free music on the street. I listen to a good blues band playing in a little park. Then I go into a hamburger joint. Sit at the counter. Four sexy young white-trash girls are at a table. I kind of eye them. This one girl in a halter top keeps lifting her arms over her head, like she's stretching. When she does it she looks at me, flashing me her oddly super-white, beautiful shaved armpits and sweet breasts.

I order a club soda and French fries. The girl with the pits comes over to me.

"Hi, I'm Jennifer," she says in her southern twang.

"I'm Jonathan."

"Are you drinking?"

"No."

"Why not?"

"Trying not to."

One of her girlfriends joins her, the other two stay at the table.

"Even though you don't drink, can you buy me and my girlfriend a drink? My sister died."

She looks right at me. I can't tell if she's lying. "I'm sorry about your sister. When did she die?"

"A week ago. I'm out partying to forget, but I tell everybody first thing we meet."

"How'd she die?"

"Car accident. Tractor-trailer drove her car off the road. . . . Can you buy us drinks?"

I order drinks for her and her girlfriend. Vodka and cranberry juice. Good for urinary tract infections and getting wasted. The drinks come in big plastic to-go cups. Eight bucks. I'm on a tight budget.

"What religion are you?" she asks me.

"No religion," I lie. I'm afraid to tell her I'm Jewish. I'm in the South, after all.

"I thought maybe you were Catholic," she says.

"Why?"

"Jonathan's a Catholic name. . . . Well, see you." She and her girlfriend suddenly leave me, their drinks in hand. I've been conned. They go out of the restaurant, onto the street. Her two other friends get up to leave. I call one of them over.

"Did your friend's sister die?"

The girl looks a little startled. But she catches on quick, that her girlfriend must have pulled a con. "Yeah, she died."

"How?"

"She was on drugs." She leaves me. I don't know what to believe. Doesn't matter. Those armpits were worth the eight bucks.

10:30 P.M.

I go to the Peabody, which is Memphis's most famous hotel. It's a grand old thing, and the lobby, which is a big bar, is packed with an unholy throng of white trash and black trash, all gathered for the fight. It's like spring break but for adults. About a thousand people are jammed into a space the size of a basketball court. The women are all wearing incredibly revealing dresses; the men are either costumed like gangsters or wearing professional sport-team tops and baggy pants.

I'm trying to spot prostitutes, but it's hard to tell the difference between the regular women and the pros. Maybe they're all pros. I do make eye contact with this one lovely woman, who is definitely on the job. She gives me a sweet smile and there's that fake shy look in her eye, as if she and I are in on the same cute joke. But it's not a cute joke. For money, she'll put her legs on my shoulders, we'll pretend to make love, and we'll both feel like hell afterward. Well, at least I will; I can't speak for her. But she is gorgeous—light brown skin and a beautiful, curvy figure. Then I see her make those same eyes to a pro basketball player, whose name I don't know, but I recognize him from watching games on TV. He walks over to the woman, they exchange a few words, and he punches her number into his cell phone. She walks off. The basketball player is then surrounded by four white girls in skimpy dresses.

"You're beautiful!" this one girl says to him. She puts her high-heeled foot next to his. "Your feet are huge!"

Friday, June 7, 11 A.M.

I go to Graceland. It's situated on a dreary four-lane highway—Elvis Presley Boulevard—which is lined on both sides with chicken places and gas stations. It must have just been a country road when he bought the house in the fifties.

On line for the tour, several sports journalists nod at me. It's like we're all in Memphis for a long wedding: you get to know people, feel friendly.

Elvis's house blows me away. I never was a huge fan before but now I am. The guy was incredible. Weird. Alive. Driven. Beautiful. I kind of feel like crying. The whole place is one big mausoleum, a wake. He tried so hard for so long—thousands of concerts, thousands of hours in recording studios and on movie sets; no way would he have wanted to die on a toilet at age forty-two from an overdose of pills.

In a museum across from the house, right at the entrance, there's a plaque that says Elvis's heroes were Rudolph Valentino and Captain Marvel, followed by this wild statement: "Everyone shares a common element with Elvis. He encompasses the daring, the familiar, the spiritual, the sexual, the masculine, the androgynous, the eccentric, the traditional, the God-like, the God-fearing, the liberal and the conservative in all of us."

On another plaque, there's a list of Elvis's posthumous accomplishments; here's one of them: "Guinness World Record—First Live Tour Starring a Performer Who Is No Longer Living." I learn that for the last four years, video concerts of Elvis have been touring around the world to sold-out crowds. And when I look at some pictures of Elvis toward the end of his life, from his Vegas years, it occurs to me that among the many dreams for himself which he made come true was that he also got to be—when he'd wear his crazy, sparkling capes—his childhood hero: Captain Marvel.

2:30 P.M.

I eat lunch at the Yellow Rose Cafe, which is on deserted Main Street. A trolley car runs up and down the street, but there are no businesses, just a few ancient cafes like the Yellow Rose. I order the catfish special, which comes with spaghetti, corn on the cob, green beans, and coleslaw. The decor of the place is circa 1972. My waitress is defeated and ancient—no top teeth. But she's sweet and the food is good. Memphis reminds me of my trip a few years ago to Havana—a place stuck in time.

4 P.M.

I'm walking around and I spot the basketball players Charles Oakley and Derrick Coleman. They're drinking beer out of plastic cups with a bunch of Memphis street people. I approach Oakley, whom I followed for years when he was with the Knicks. The guy is so damn tall that it's supernatural. I don't know if I should call him Mr. Oakley or Charles. Is it rude to call him by his first name when I don't know him?

Oakley is talking to a homeless guy whose mouth looks like it has exploded. "What the hell happened to your lip?" Oakley asks the man.

"I had a seizure," says the man.

"A seizure. Damn. That's nasty. Get that shit fixed."

The man with the exploded lip walks off. "Excuse me, Mr. Oakley," I say, "can I ask you a few questions? I'm with a New York paper."

He peers down at me from far away. My head comes up to his nipples, and I'm nearly six feet tall. "What do you want to know?" he says.

"Who do you think is going to win, Tyson or Lewis?"

"Don't want to answer no questions about the fight. Here to have a good time." Coleman is by his side. They're both staring at me and sipping from their beer.

"How about the Nets-Lakers then?" I ask.

"Lakers in four."

"Even with Jason Kidd?"

"I like Kidd but David Stern doesn't." David Stern is the commissioner of the NBA. This seems a curious thing to say.

"How come David Stern doesn't like Jason Kidd?" I ask.

Oakley scowls at me. "No more questions. You better watch out, man. You're the only white person around here. Get out of here." He steps toward me, and so does Coleman.

"Yeah, get out of here," Coleman says. Their hostility feels completely uncalled-for and strange. I slink off. White and humiliated.

10 P.M.

I go to another baseball game and then stagger about the steaming-hot town. Memphis is in a complete frenzy now. Everyone is running around, trying to spot someone famous.

You hear shrieks and screams up and down the streets when a celebrity like Dikembe Mutumbo or Magic Johnson or a rap star is seen. I come upon twenty black girls all dressed exactly alike—blue terry cloth minishorts and minitops. I ask one of the girls, "Are you some kind of group or team?"

"No."

"You just all dress alike?"

"Yeah, we're all friends. We came down from Milwaukee to party."

"Who are you rooting for?"

"Mike Tyson."

Most everyone I ask is rooting for Tyson and predicts that he will win. It's the best story line. People want him to have a second chance. It's projection: We all want second chances. At everything. We all want to prove Fitzgerald wrong that there are no second acts in American life. Larry Merchant, an HBO announcer, said to me earlier in the day, "Tyson is trying to redeem his whole life with this one fight."

I go to the Peabody and it is more packed tonight than last night. I'm hitting that point when you're traveling by yourself and the despair kicks in and you start craving to be with a friend. But it's nearly impossible to make a friend when you're on the road; hell, it's practically impossible to make friends with my own friends when I'm home in New York City.

Saturday, June 8, 11 A.M.

I'm in the lobby of my hotel drinking the bad coffee and waiting for a taxi. A thick, heavyset man with a bald head is also drinking coffee.

"You here for the fight?" he asks me.

"Yes," I say.

"Who do you like?"

"I can't imagine that Tyson can do it. But maybe; he's got that punch."

"Nah, he won't do it. He's only fought tomato cans the last few years. . . . You need tickets?"

"No, I'm covering it for a newspaper."

"What paper?"

"A New York weekly, *New York Press.*"

"I'm from New York, too," he says. "Long Island . . . So, listen, I got a problem. You know anybody that wants tickets?"

"No," I say.

"Yeah, well, I got ten thousand dollars' worth in my pocket that I have to sell. I was on the streets last night. The Peabody. But nobody with big money is out there. You should write about that. White corporate America didn't come. Three reasons. Turned off by boxing in general. Didn't know if Tyson would do something. And the town. It's a black town."

It hits me that this guy is Mafia. He asks me if he can borrow my cell phone. I give it to him.

"Anthony, no luck," he says into my phone. "I'm going to the airports, hit people when they come off the planes. Then I'll go to the casinos, then the stadium. . . . Right . . . I'll call you."

He gives me back my phone. "Listen," he says to me. "You're a writer, right? I have this idea for a sports cartoon; I want to sell it. I called the YES network but they blew me off, fucking bastards."

He tells me the idea; it's actually really good. "So you want to roll up your sleeves," he says after spelling out the concept, "and get to work with me on this? I need a writer for the dialogue."

A Mafia guy is proposing I work with him. I tell him I have no experience with cartoons. He looks at me disappointed.

"I'm sorry I can't help you," I say. "But it's a really good idea."

His taxi comes. We shake hands good-bye.

2 P.M.

I go to the National Civil Rights Museum, which has been built out of the Lorraine Motel where Martin Luther King Jr. was shot April 4, 1968. Like Elvis's house, the place has been preserved just as it was—two late-sixties cars rest in the parking lot, the original motel sign still stands, and you can look up at the second-floor railing where King was killed. Strange: Two Kings died in this town. No wonder it has the blues.

There's a modern edition built onto the motel's structure and after walking through galleries that portray the history of civil rights, you come to the room where King spent his last night, which you can look at through a glass partition. His bed is left unmade.

Martin Luther King Jr. was only thirty-nine years old when he was murdered, and I'm struck by how young he was. Throughout the museum you can hear tapes of his rich, beautiful voice—the speeches and sermons he gave.

There's a plaque outside the motel, beneath his room, like a gravestone. It reads: "*They said one to another, behold, here cometh the dreamer. . . . Let us slay him. . . . And we shall see what becomes of his dreams.*"—Genesis 37:19–20.

9:45 P.M.

I walk around the floor of the arena. I see Denzel Washington, Magic Johnson, George Foreman, Cuba Gooding Jr., Matt Dillon, Samuel Jackson, Joe Frazier, Montel Williams, Laila Ali (very beautiful), Morgan Freeman, Val Kilmer, and David Hasselhoff, to name a few. But it's like they're all my friends, so I get no thrill out of spotting them. I do get Vince McMahon's autograph for my son, which is nice. Then I approach David Remnick.

"Excuse me, Mr. Remnick," I say. "Can I ask you a few questions? I'm with *New York Press*."

"Oh, sure."

"Who do you like?"

"Do you want the rationalist answer or the Nietzschean? The rationalist says Lewis. Tyson hasn't had a good fight in years, and Lewis has sufficient skill to keep Tyson away. But he can't afford to make mistakes the way Tyson can, which you can do when you have a punch like Tyson's."

"And the Nietzschean?"

"Tyson."

"Why? Because he's beyond good and evil?"

"Yes, he's crazy."

10:15 P.M.

I've snuck down from my $1,400 seats to $2,500 seats. I'm about a hundred feet from the ring. Tyson enters the arena. The crowd of about sixteen thousand is on their feet and screaming primal bloody murder. It feels like a massive gang rape is about to take place and we're all the rapists and the victims at the same time. I've smoked crack, and the energy in the arena is like they lit a bonfire of crack in the ring and we're all breathing the fumes. My heart feels like it's ready to ejaculate itself out of my chest. The place is seething, gladiatorial, rabid.

Lewis comes into the arena with his coterie, and then he climbs into the ring. He and Tyson are separated by a phalanx of yellow-shirted security guards. There won't be the traditional touching of gloves. All precautions have been taken so that Tyson doesn't do anything to cost everyone millions of dollars—like throw a punch *before* the first bell is struck.

Then the first bell is struck. Tyson comes out swinging. He charges like a bull, his squat body launching these missiles which are his arms. Lewis evades and wraps Tyson up, but gets hit a few times. We're all scared. There's mayhem before our eyes. But Lewis is formidable; he lands a few shots, slows Tyson down. He holds Tyson around the neck, which will tire him out. That happened in my little amateur fight. Three minutes race by. The first round is over. Tyson has won the round, but Lewis is not dead. This seems a triumph.

But that round, it turns out, is all Mike Tyson has in him. After that Lewis repeatedly smashes him in the face with his left jab. Tyson's head keeps snapping back violently like something out of a *Rocky* movie. By the third round, I begin to feel quite sorry for Tyson. His face and brain are getting pummeled. He absorbs almost every punch Lewis throws. Every now and then he unleashes a flurry of punches, some life in him wanting to emerge, but by the fifth round, he stops punching and just takes a beating. His face is battered, disfigured.

In the eighth round he takes a shot to his head, which sends his Brooklyn-born brain flying hard against the inside of his skull. He crumples. Concussed. But he's half-standing. Lewis gives him a shove down to the canvas, so he won't have to hit Tyson anymore. Tyson lies there, and puts his hand to his face, like a child covering a wound, ashamed and injured and overwhelmed.

Several minutes later he is standing and is being interviewed with Lewis. He reaches up and wipes his own blood off Lewis's face. It's his best punch of the night: a tender gesture.

1:15 A.M.

After my debacle on the fence, I'm in Discretions watching a sexy middle-aged black couple dance. All of the other couples, about five, are unattractive white people in their fifties. Two women, who look like the kind of ladies you see playing bingo, are playfully pinching each other's nipples and laughing. They have their feet in their men's crotches. Every place in Memphis is packed to the gills, but this joint is nearly empty, except for these aging swingers. What the hell have I stumbled into? There's a sign that says, *No Sex on the Premises.*

The black lady on the dance floor hikes up her orange skirt and her man gets behind her and rubs against her beautiful ass. I sip my club soda. They finish their dance. The man comes up to me, "Would you like to dance with my girlfriend?"

"Yes," I say, shocked.

She gives me the same treatment. Lifts that orange skirt. She's in her late forties, but hot. She's wearing a thong and has an ass like two halves of a bowling ball. Life is good sometimes. I figure her boyfriend likes to watch. She treats me very nicely. I do worry that I dance like a white boy. But I am a white boy. The dance comes to an end. I thank her and buy the two of them drinks. There's no invitation to come home with them or even join them for the drinks I bought them, so I sit back at my table and a few more songs play and they start dancing again. They don't ask me to join, but I'm not hurt. It's incredible that I got to dance with her even once. So I get the hell out of there. I have to find a taxi, get to the motel, pack up, and catch a 5:30 A.M. plane.

I walk for two hours and nearly lose my mind: No taxis are free. Plenty of hookers on the street are free, but not really free. I've never seen so many prostitutes in my life. Finally, around 4 A.M., I get a cab. I'm going to have to go to the hotel, get my bag, and head right to the airport. The driver says to me, "I've been working twenty-four hours and I'm not stopping. We may never see something like this again in Memphis."

"I think you're right," I say, and I look out the window to the black morning sky, but if I was being poetic, I'd say it was dark blue.

2002

New-thumb-of-thought (noo-thum-uv-thot), n. The advancement in the human brain, first noticed in 2017 in Bloomington, Indiana. Just as man had once developed a thumb and vastly improved his lot and several thousand generations later could get into good schools as a result, so too did another advancement take place: not in the area of the hand, but in the back lobe of the human brain. For years people had talked about the "frontal lobe," and all the while the back lobe was busy trying to improve itself in a Darwinian fashion, and so it did. The advancement was a brain—led by its backside—which recognized the virtues of a vegan diet, good manners, and tai chi as a means of pollution-free space-and-time-travel. This new brain also led to the happy discovery of Atlantis City as an underwater gaming emporium where everyone won but didn't care. This back-lobe brain's abilities were called a *new-thumb-of-thought*, and its effects were felt worldwide within fifty years. People flew through the air doing their tai chi, sometimes staying in the present, sometimes visiting the future or the past, which was how Atlantis was refound—during someone's trip back in time. This new brain also allowed people to swim underwater without breathing, so that there was no more drowning, upsetting the Lifeguard Union, but they got with the program and didn't complain. This underwater ability also helped, it should be noted, with the Atlantis discovery. And, as indicated, everyone became vegans and wrote thank-you notes to each other; and all religions, due to the advent of pleasant manners, were nicely fused. McDonald's, since there were so many of them, were now used as cow shrines, which pleased the Hindus. Sue Schwartz-Miller, an African-American-Jewish-Baptist woman from Bloomington, is credited with being the gene-carrier for the first brain which possessed the *new-thumb-of-thought*. She was observed in 2017 floating over Indiana University doing her tai chi and as a result became a big TV star. Her earnings on TV then allowed her to have many children—eighteen to be exact—so that her brain and its great gene quickly spread through the United States and the rest of the world.

ESCAPE HOME

I am the prodigal son who didn't get very far. I grew up in northern New Jersey—the *banlieue* of New York—and now I live in Brooklyn. I am separated from my parents by about fifty miles, but, really, there's almost no distance between us— I speak to them nearly every day. They like to hear my voice, they say, and always the two of them are on the phone together. They're kind of a Siamese couple. They've been married nearly fifty years.

Maybe because we speak so often, I don't go home that much. But when I do, I always take the same route, as I did the other day: the F to Manhattan, which came for me immediately, as it usually does—I'd like to think I have magic with the F, though it's probably just frequent service. Just before the F arrived, I saw the rails light up with the glow of the train's headlights. I always look for this, this light at the beginning of the tunnel—it's my augury of the train's arrival, and the rails look beautiful when they are illuminated.

So I took the F to the West Fourth Street station and then I walked to the Path train, which is on Ninth Street. The Path took a while. It's never as attentive to my needs as the F, and the platform, with its low ceiling and smudged brick tiles, was its usual gloomy, subterranean self.

Eventually, the Path train arrived and we proceeded to careen under the West Village and then the Hudson River, until we emerged in Hoboken, New Jersey. I climbed the stairs to the train station, which, like an old brass statue, has turned green-blue from time and water. The station is straight out of European central casting: no roof above the dozen or more tracks, the sky visible above the long trains, conductors in blue uniforms, a grand waiting room with oak benches, people bustling, clocks announcing. It always reminds me of the Gare d'Austerlitz in Paris—if only I was catching a train to Rome each time I went there instead of Bergen County, New Jersey.

But Bergen County also has its charms. It's where my parents always wait for me at the Ridgewood station to take me home, a few towns away, to Oakland. I rent my apartment in Brooklyn, but I don't have a *home.* My parents are still my home. I am part of a vast generation of people who live perpetually as if they have just graduated from college. I am thirty-eight years old. I wear a backpack and have no savings. I console myself with the thought that people live longer nowadays so it makes sense that some of us take longer to mature.

So I don't have my own home, but going to my parents is a chance to time-travel, to dip into the past, into my life— the only thing I really possess, or that anyone possesses, if I may speak universally. It's also a chance to love my parents, which as I get older, seems more and more important.

This bit of time travel takes only forty minutes on the train, first through the Meadowlands—amidst the refineries, beautiful fields of light-brown stalks waver, like something out of Kansas—and then through the leafy towns of Bergen County.

During this recent train ride to Ridgewood, I sat next to a young woman talking on her cell phone to a friend. "I'm on the train going home," she said. "I mean to my parents' house. But I still call it home." She laughed self-consciously into her phone. I knew what she was saying.

My parents were waiting at the station—my mother beaming, my father stoic but inwardly happy. I kissed them. We drove home. My parents have lived in the same house for forty-two years. As we turned onto our street, my mother said, as she has dozens of times before: "I always think how you said once, 'Do you ever wonder how many times you've driven down this street?'"

"I know, Mom," I whined, like a child. "I said that years ago and now every time we come down the street, you tell me I said that. The new question is: How many times have you wondered how many times you've come down this street? One of these days we have to get a calculator and put an end to this discussion!"

My mother laughed sweetly. She's tolerant of her impatient, ironic son. We turned onto our driveway. Our house is on a little pond. There was end-of-the-day light. It was very beautiful. The water on the pond was emerald, reflecting the trees. The neighborhood was quiet—the kind of quiet you don't hear in New York. We went into the house and I took my backpack to *my room.*

Then dinner. We talked, as usual, of my sister and her children in California. Then my mother worked on photo albums and my father and I watched two movies on TV, discussing the plots and the actors.

When we called it a night, my father said, "I liked watching those movies with you." He and I have come a long way since our frequent restaging of *Oedipus* during my adolescence. I hugged him and my mother good night. Then I got into my old bed and I slept well. I dreamt that I was home.

2002

NO CONTACT, ASSHOLE!

The summer of 1990 was a bad one. It should have been a good one but it was a bad one. I've pulled a lot of stunts in my day, mostly of the sick sexual variety, but that summer I reached a new low. Or a new high. It was so low it was high, if you know what I mean.

I was twenty-six and a single parent. My son was four. He smelled good all the time, the way little kids do.

So my son was real cute. Red hair, blue eyes, ivory skin. Full of love. I had him for the whole summer.

We stayed with my parents in New Jersey. I needed their help with looking after my son for such a long stretch. Because I was a writer and made my living driving a taxi, I could just take off, so I did—all of July and August.

About two mornings each week, I'd go to the library to try to write from nine to twelve, and my mother would look after my son. I felt guilty about those three hours, but I needed to work a little.

Around week five, I started to come unhinged. I had no social life, I was playing with my son twelve hours a day in the humid Jersey weather, and on the two mornings I went to the library my writing was lousy. Also, my father was still working back then, so he was tormented and insane and we weren't getting along. So, like I said, I was coming unhinged, which means I had to do something, take action. And taking action usually means hurting myself.

So one day my son was taking a nap and I was looking at the local free throwaway newspaper and I spotted a curious ad in the classifieds: a dominatrix with a transsexual assistant was offering $100 one-hour sessions. What the hell was this doing in a throwaway newspaper in suburban New Jersey?

Naturally, I called the number.

A youngish sounding woman answered the phone. "What do you want?" she said.

"I'm calling about your ad," I said in a whispery voice.

"Yeah, so? You want a session, faggot?"

She was already in character. "Yes," I said.

"When do you want to see me, faggot?"

I told her what time I could get together and the girl laid down the law. She'd meet me the next day at 11 A.M. at T.G.I. Friday's, just off the local highway. I was to stand at the bar and have a pack of unopened Marlboro cigarettes in my hand. If she didn't like the looks of me, she'd turn right around. If I passed inspection, she'd come over to me and ask for a cigarette. I wasn't to give her one, but follow her out to her car, where she'd blindfold me and drive me to her house. It was all very noir, metaphorically and otherwise.

"Do I have to be blindfolded?" I asked.

"You think I'm going to let a freak like you know where I live?" She was very mean on the phone, but I figured she was just being professional. A professional dominatrix, that is. They're supposed to be mean.

The next day I was at the T.G.I. Friday's by ten-fifty with a pack of Marlboros. My mother thought I was at the library. I should have been with my son. I'm a terrible person.

The place had just opened when I got there. I ordered a coffee. At eleven she walked in—very short, maybe five-one, brunette, pretty, early twenties, jeans and a halter top, sunglasses. We played the cigarette game, then out to her car. My heart was explosive. She didn't have a blindfold but sunglasses that were taped over.

"I don't want a cop stopping me because he sees that I have a faggot like you blindfolded," she explained. If I was lucky, she'd kill me fast and dump my body in the Meadowlands. My poor parents; my poor son.

I kept trying to peer out the bottom of the sunglasses to see where I was being taken to be murdered. Despite my nervousness, I asked her lots of questions. She was pretty forthcoming. I've always been good with the Q&A.

She was Italian-Catholic. Ever since she was a teenager she had gotten off on dominating men, especially since all men were assholes. Her high school boyfriend was her transsexual assistant; she had been feminizing him for a few years, feeding him hormone pills, making him dress like a girl, and, though he resisted at first, he was now happy with his transformation. Eventually, they'd have his penis cut off and they'd be lesbian lovers.

The whole thing was so sick it was thrilling. She and this guy were actually living out a dream that millions—well, maybe thousands—of perverts wanted. And I had found her in a throwaway newspaper!

She told me that when she and her boy/girlfriend had enough money saved they were going to move to New York and open a first-class dungeon. Then from the dungeon they'd get enough money for his sex-change operation.

I got all this in a twenty-minute car ride, which I think involved her driving around in circles, in case I was peering out the bottom of the glasses. I felt like James Bond being kidnapped.

We pulled into a driveway; she took me by the hand and led me into a house, which I could perceive from the bottom of my glasses. Then we went down some stairs and she removed my glasses. We were in a carpeted basement room which was just about empty—there was a radio, a futon mattress, and a big box with S&M paraphernalia. A pole ran from the floor to the ceiling and all the walls were mirrored. I gave her the hundred bucks. Then she slapped me and led me to the pole. She took some rope from her S&M box and she tied my wrists behind my back and around the pole. She slapped me again and then left me alone in the room. It was nearly eleven-thirty. I told my mother I'd meet her at twelve-thirty at the lake where we took my son swimming. I was going to be late!

She left me tied to that pole for ten minutes. I imagined this was part of the torture, but I thought it was a rip-off, so I managed to free myself, just like James Bond. I tried the door. It was locked. I could have busted it down, but I didn't: My

James Bondness went only so far. Then she came into the room dressed in black bra, panties, stockings, boots—usual dominatrix garb—and slapped me for slipping my bonds. Her slaps stung but weren't bad. Then she put the radio on, WPLJ. I had been listening to that station my whole life, but never in the basement of a dominatrix.

"What are you into?" she asked. "Want me to flog you?"

"Can I kiss your breasts?" I asked. She looked pretty in her bra.

"No contact, asshole," she said, and then she slapped me again—contact!—and looked at me like I was crazy. But I didn't want to be flogged. I wanted to nurse on her breasts and maybe lick her pussy. I wasn't an S&M nut; I was just a nut. My perversion is that I try everything once, even if I'm not into it.

Then her tranny boyfriend—a tall, slender brunette wearing a negligee—came in and gave me a wide-eyed north/south. I wasn't bad-looking back then and so I think he was attracted to me.

The girl had the tranny undress me, and then they conferred in the corner while I stood there naked.

Then the tranny came over and started rubbing against me, trying to slow-dance with me to the music coming from the radio, and I didn't mind—he was a pretty good-looking girl. And I knew what was going on: I was being tossed to the tranny-slave like a piece of meat and the girl was getting off on watching.

Then the tranny stopped dancing, got a strawberry-flavored condom from the S&M box, and knelt down in front of me to give me a blow job. He rolled the sugar-coated condom on me and before he took me in his mouth, the girl came over and slapped me violently. It hurt. The other slaps had been warm-ups. She went to do it again, but I caught her wrist this time and bent her arm behind her back. She was a little thing, even in her black boots. The tranny just stayed on his knees, wide-eyed. I held the girl's arm behind her back, and slow-danced her from behind. My penis, in the condom, pressed against her ass. That vicious slap had done something to me, turned me into Robert Mitchum. The girl didn't say anything; I think she was stunned. Maybe she liked having the tables turned. The tranny watched and smiled. Poor nutty slave. He was going to lose his dick someday.

Well, after that, things got a little sordid. An unlit candle—in lieu of a dildo—somehow entered the picture and the three of us rolled around on that futon. At some point the girl did flog me two or three times, but I let her—I'm not a ungenerous lover and I had to build her esteem back up after I had manhandled her.

Then it ended the way these things usually end: Somebody gets a paper towel and you wish you had never been born. The tranny said to me, "I hope you'll see us again. You're beautiful."

I got dressed and the girl made me put the sunglasses back on. She drove me to the T.G.I. Friday's in five minutes, confirming my suspicions about the circular method she had used on the way over. She dropped me off and didn't say good-bye. It was a sunny day. One shouldn't do such things on sunny days. I don't know how the perverts in California live with themselves.

I got to the swimming hole fifteen minutes late. My mother assumed that I had been working well in the library.

I took my son into the water and we were quickly joined by several other four-year-olds. I was the only dad around and so I was like a pied piper for the kids. They were crawling all over me, playing and splashing. At some point, my son was really bouncing on my back and it hurt and for a moment I wondered why and then I remembered. My brief flogging had bruised me.

To be able to live with myself, I had immediately, upon getting into my car at T.G.I. Friday's, blocked from my mind the lurid scene I had just engaged in, but then with my son bouncing on my bruises I couldn't forget what had happened and I felt wildly ashamed. In retrospect it doesn't seem so terrible—so I cavorted with a dominatrix and a pre-op transsexual. What harm, really, was done? Isn't it a sort of funny story all these years later? Time softens everything, I guess. But in that moment, I was disgusted that my beautiful son should come in contact with those bruises. Why am I like this? I thought. What is wrong with me? I hated myself, but I had to *love him.*

So I kept playing in the water. To keep going and not lose my mind, I had to pretend that I was a good person—the generous pied piper. It was the only way to cope, and it seemed to work—my son and all the other children were laughing and happy, and my mother sat in her beach chair proud of her son and her grandchild. I played with the children for hours. It was a beautiful day.

2002

WHORES, WRITERS, AND
A PIMPLE: MY TRIP TO EUROPE

November 7

I went to Europe to promote my memoir *What's Not to Love?* in the Netherlands, and my novels *The Extra Man* and *I Pass Like Night* in Germany. My first stop was Amsterdam. I felt very lucky and privileged to be going on such a great trip—a book tour in Europe! I was so pleased and honored, but little did I know at the start of my journey that a colossal pimple would undermine the whole thing.

In Amsterdam, my hotel was called the Ambassade, a former seventeenth-century residence located on the Herengracht, one of the many pretty canals that ring the beautiful city like the circles of a tree. When I checked in it was two-thirty in the morning according to my body clock, but eight-thirty in the morning according to more important clocks, and I was too wired to sleep, anyway, and so I had some breakfast.

Sitting in the dining room of the hotel was a man who bore a striking resemblance to the writer Ian McEwan— greasy, gray-black hair, thick glasses, and a drawn, clerkish face. But I thought, It can't be Ian McEwan.

So I didn't say anything to the man, and what would I have said anyway? I've only read one of McEwan's novels, which I liked very much; it was his first, *The Cement Garden.* But complimenting him on that book would be like the time I saw John Updike in a deli in Brooklyn and complimented him on his second novel, *The Centaur,* the only book of his I've read, thus ignoring years of output, and I didn't want to make the same mistake if this was McEwan. Later, I learned it was indeed him, that almost all foreign writers who come to Amsterdam stay at the Ambassade, but I didn't see him again and it's just as well.

After breakfast I slept for a little while and then had two interviews about *What's Not to Love?* I felt embarrassed that while the world is going mad—destruction of the environment, hatred between cultures—that journalists should be spending their time on a subject like yours truly, though, of course, I hadn't balked at the chance for a free trip for yours truly, one of the points of which was to talk to journalists. So I felt mildly ashamed about the whole thing, but in some ways it's reassuring that the world—at least some parts—wants to continue its middle-class pursuit of reading books and reading articles about people who write books.

Thus, I answered the interviewers' questions as playfully as I could, making sure to let them know that I am simply a literary clown and my goal is to bring some laughs to people, that perhaps this has some value and meaning in our world, whatever it is that value and meaning mean, if you know what I mean.

One interviewer then asked me if I was a Shakespearean clown—one who tells the truth—or just a circus clown, and I wasn't sure what to say, though my ego, I must admit, liked the notion of being a Shakespearean clown. But I said that I was a circus clown, adding that circus clowns are not without gravitas, especially since they provoke a whole phobia— coulrophobia, which is described as a persistent and abnormal fear of clowns.

Another interviewer asked me why I wrote an autobiography, and I said it was an auto-*erotic*-biography since there's so much in the book about masturbation, but despite his excellent English he didn't seem to get the joke.

That afternoon, I walked around Amsterdam, and it was very lovely and so bourgeois: everyone riding on bicycles or taking trams, numerous cafes and gourmet shops—all of it just so incredibly pleasant. So I couldn't help but think, as many have before me, which is probably why I thought it, how the Europeans really have mastered the middle-class existence.

In the evening, I attended the opening performances of Crossing Borders, the literature and music festival that I was a part of, and I attended the concert of a huge Sicilian funeral band. The American equivalent would be a high school marching band, especially since these Italians usually play while parading down the streets of Sicily in pageants celebrating/mourning a death.

After the band played half a dozen dirges, they gave up

the stage for Werner Fassbinder's former muse, Hanna Schygulla, and she did a strange, eerie musical theater piece, singing and talking in many languages, like something out of *Star Trek*. At one point she said in whispery, accented English, "Men kill what they love."

I wondered if this was really true; after all, Fassbinder supposedly loved her and she was still alive. Or maybe he didn't love her and that's why she was still alive.

Anyway, after these strange performances, I went and walked around the famous Red Light District and found it to be quite disenchanting. There were hundreds of women behind these body-length windows and you could peer at them in their little cells as they sat on stools, and behind them there was usually a dreary cot with a dreary towel. If a cell was occupied, a curtain would be drawn. And while many of the women had beautiful bodies, their faces were destroyed.

Last year, as a journalist, I watched the filming of a porn video in California, and seeing these Amsterdam prostitutes I thought of what the head of lighting on the porn set had said to me about young porn actresses after they've been in the business a while: "They get that whore face. A face that's seen too much."

Well, these Amsterdam women had that face. Even if their features were beautiful they were ugly, though "ugly" is not quite the right word. Maybe "dead" is the right word. Their faces were dead. They had seen too much and *they had been seen too much.* Every night thousands of drunken tourists promenade through the narrow corridors of the Red Light District and gawk at these women like they're exhibits in a freak show, and being looked at that way must do something to you. And of course, there's the job itself: sucking on hundreds, if not thousands, of terrible cocks every year, or having the men on top of you with their stinking bodies, fucking your vagina or your ass.

Nevertheless, I compulsively walked through all of the alleyways of the district, looking at scores of women. Many of the alleyways formed a kind of ghetto, with only black women available down certain passages.

As I walked about, I wanted to find at least one woman I was attracted to, one who didn't have a face that was dead. It was like I was trolling the beach at the ocean, hoping to come across one perfect intact shell. And I did eventually find one young girl who didn't look destroyed. She was small and dark and very pretty. She was probably from one of the old Dutch colonies in the Philippines. After I saw her, beautiful shell found but not collected, I was able to leave the alleyways and get back to my hotel.

November 8

I did more interviews in the morning and the afternoon—why do you write about the "Mangina"[6] was a frequent query— and then in the evening, in a smoky theater which held about two hundred people, I gave a performance on the same bill as the very funny and very famous David Sedaris.

---

[6] The "Mangina" is a friend of mine who invented a prosthetic vagina called the Mangina, which he wears on occasion as some kind of ongoing performance-art piece and as penance for having lost the love of his life some years before. His invention is called the Mangina and he's called the Mangina. To read about him, feel free to consult my book *What's Not to Love?* and its sequel, which also features him, *My Less Than Secret Life.*

When I came off the stage to nice applause, I was in the middle of a sea of people, kind well-wishers, and then the sea parted just a little, and I was approached by an older, sexy woman in a shawl. She pressed a card on me. "We should meet up in New York and talk about doing something together," she said. I looked down at the card: Xavier Hollander. The name didn't register at first, but then it hit me. "I used to read you all the time in *Penthouse* as a young boy. It's an honor to meet you," I gushed. It was the Happy Hooker herself. Her face *wasn't* dead and she smiled at me, stroked my cheek with her hand, and said, "We'll meet in New York," and then she disappeared back into the crowd, in the direction of the exit. What she was doing in Amsterdam I had no idea, though I later learned that Amsterdam is her home.

That night I stayed out late with all the people from my publishing house and they drank beer after beer and smoked cigarette after cigarette, and I absorbed enough secondhand smoke to give myself, Mayor Bloomberg, and all the five boroughs of New York City cancer.[7]

November 9

In the morning, I did something unusual: I made an appointment at this place called Koan Float, where I could go into a sensory deprivation tank. I'd always wanted to try one of those and the place was right next to my hotel.

---

[7] At the time, 2002, Mayor Bloomberg was pursuing his goal of banning smoking in all restaurants, bars, and businesses, a goal that he achieved in 2003.

Here's how it worked: I got my own room with a shower and a tank, the attendant gave me instructions to put Vaseline over any open cuts, and I was left alone in the room.

I showered off and climbed naked into the powder-blue tank, which looked like the backside of an extinct AMC Pacer, a doomed car which I always admired for its fat ass. The tank was filled with about two feet of warm salt water. I then pulled the hatch down and was in complete darkness. There were buttons along the wall of the tank for lights, music, intercom—in case you started to panic you could contact the girl at the front desk—but I preferred to be in darkness without musical accompaniment.

I lay on my back and the salt water buoyed me up. Immediately, there was a terrible stinging in my ass, which has been itchy for about fifteen years now. I don't know what the hell the problem is down there.

My ass was probably stinging in the salt water because I'm always irritating it by scratching it. I have two very bad habits—I scratch my ass and I pick my nose. The worst is when I pick my nose after I scratch my ass, having forgotten that I've scratched my ass, and I wonder why my finger smells like I've changed a diaper, and then I remember and I sort of wish in those moments that somebody would just come along and shoot me, and then I wonder if other people have fingers laced with feces, other people like chefs and waiters. Anyway, I really shouldn't be let out of the house, let alone sent all the way to civilized Europe.

Well, after about ten minutes in the tank my ass stopped stinging and I went into a profound meditative state. These deprivation tanks are real meditation shortcuts. I was counting my breaths as I floated, and I traveled back in time to when I used to do Zen meditation twenty years ago at Princeton as a freshman, inspired by Kerouac's *Dharma Bums* and my desire to have a Beat experience, despite being at Princeton, a preppy way station and not exactly the Jack Kerouac School of Disembodied Poetics.

After forty minutes I came out of the tank—the girl informed me over the intercom that my time was up—and I was blissfully happy. I walked along the gorgeous Amsterdam canals and wondered why I ever have worries in life. All anxiety and persistent feelings of doom had been leeched out of me by that tank. I was euphoric. It was beautiful!

Well, the gods were observing me, because right at the zenith of my happiness I stepped in a huge wet pile of diarrhea dog shit, which is such a cliché, but it actually happened. This, however, didn't dent my delightful spiritual state. What dented my state was that I ate an enormous breakfast at the hotel after the tank experience and I felt like my gut was going to burst. On top of everything else in life—ass-scratching and nose-picking addictions—I sometimes have IBS and had been nervously waiting for my stomach to detonate on this trip and wreak havoc.

And now the moment had arrived. IBS is kind of like having a terrorist network in your very own intestines: You never know when you might explode. So I rushed out of the dining room and up four flights to my room, and the maid was there! Cleaning the bathroom! This was too cruel!

I sat on my bed and pretended to read a book while she rinsed the tub. I didn't know if my sphincter was going to make it, and I was unsure if there was a toilet in the lobby four floors below. I decided that the best course of action was to keep waiting there in the room. Inside my gut, I was rechanneling something quite ferocious. About five excruciating minutes passed and I didn't know how much longer I could hold out.

Finally, after about eight minutes, the maid left, and like Tiger Woods sinking a clutch putt, I got my pants down without incident—such moments in my life are my only chances at athletic heroism and sangfroid—and I sat on the toilet and blew myself up.

It's really hard to have dignity and feel good about yourself when such things occur. But about twenty minutes later some kind of amnesia sets in and you forget what happened in the bathroom, and you resume your life, hoping for the best.

That evening I gave another reading with David Sedaris, as well as several Dutch authors and an American writer named Mark Danieleski. After the reading, I spoke to Danieleski, author of *House of Leaves*, which I haven't yet had the chance to read, but it looks fascinating and the reviews have been excellent.

Despite not having read his book, I was anxious to talk to Danieleski, because I went to school with his sister, the rock singer Po, and I once saw her in a school play in which she appeared, quite memorably, without her shirt on. Why this made me eager to talk to him is a bit unclear. I guess I felt compelled to point out the odd coincidence that I vaguely knew his sister a long time ago and here we were reading together in some literary festival in Amsterdam.

So we talked. Turns out he had come with his sister to hear me read in 1989, but had forgotten my name and face, which is perfectly understandable, but it was all coming back to him now, and then the conversation moved on to our mutual American publisher, and I felt the chip on my shoulder inflame. Like most writers, I have a herpeslike chip on my shoulder when it comes to publishers. And it's like herpes, because I'll have it the rest of my life. No author is without such a chip, and it is simply this—every writer feels like their publisher doesn't do enough, and that other writers get more attention.

So it wasn't Danieleski's fault, but I found myself growing sullen. Then he went on to regale me with this tale of the elaborate American book tour our publisher had sent him on, and even though here I was in Europe on a book tour, I felt jealous. I've never been sent on a tour by an American publisher and the chip on my shoulder grew even more inflamed. I had no reason to be envious, but I was. And I guess because of the envy, I now noticed that he had a largish lump on his forehead, like half a Ping-Pong ball was under his skin.

Danieleski is a handsome fellow—looks, in fact, a lot like D. H. Lawrence—but I began to stare at this lump. Well, our conversation petered out, probably because I was focusing on the ball in the middle of his forehead, and we went our separate ways.

Later that night, I watched a band with David Sedaris and his boyfriend, Hugh—there were all sorts of bands playing at Crossing Borders, mostly at this space-age performance center called the Milkyway—and Sedaris told me that earlier he'd seen this singer who had an enormous growth on the back of his neck, like a fat maroon snake, but that nobody seemed to care, that the singer was surrounded by groupies after his set. Sedaris wondered if the fellow had become a rock star on purpose, since only rock stars could get away with growths like that. I then held forth on my confusion about neck and cheek goiters: How could goiters get so big and what was in them? And furthermore, why weren't they nipped in the bud before they became impossible to remove?

Sedaris appreciated my speech on goiters, and then I said, thinking there was an opening for such a remark, "Did you notice that Mark Danieleski had a sort of growth-lump on his forehead?"

It was a mean thing for me to say, a reaction to Danieleski's story about his book tour, and Sedaris said he hadn't noticed any lump-growth. Then we went into this bar in the Milkyway and Danieleski was there and I elbowed Sedaris, indicating that he should check out the lump.

The three of us talked for a little while, and then I left with Sedaris and said, "Did you see that lump? What do you think it is?"

"I think it's just a bruise," said Sedaris.

"I think it's a lump. It's too perfectly round to be a bruise, like there's a Super Ball under the skin," I said.

"I think it's just a bruise," said Sedaris, holding his ground, and I felt foolish and petty.

Then Sedaris had to leave with Hugh, and feeling lonely and mildly insane, I went to the Red Light District to go to this bar I had read about. I forget its exact name, but I think it was called the Banana Bar. I had read that women did depraved things with bananas in there and thought I should witness such a thing at least once in my life, having often been told tales about similar bars in Bangkok where ladies play Ping-Pong with their vaginas, which makes sense since the Asians are very good at that sport.

Anyway, I paid forty euros, roughly forty dollars, to get into the Banana Bar, and I have to say that Europe seems somewhat neutered having only one currency now, but they say change is good, even if the change—in this case, coinage—isn't very pretty. So those forty euros bought me an hour in the place and all I could drink, though since I don't imbibe anymore that part of the deal was lost on me.

The joint had two levels, each with a bar, and the place was packed with drunk British fellows. The bars were actually stages, and on each bar there were five naked women handing out drinks from a squatting or sitting position, and so while they served drinks men looked right into these nice ladies' vaginas. These women were all of a similar body type: big and voluptuous, with wide asses and pendulous breasts, shaved genitals, and shiny seal-like skin. They all seemed to be in their middle to late thirties, and it was a politically correct and diversified assembly, since there were representatives of all the races—white, black, Asian.

Unlike the girls in the windows on the street, these ladies were merry, laughing, vulgar, and bawdy, like something out of Chaucer with bodies by Brueghel.

In addition to serving drinks, the women performed a variety of lewd acts, each woman seeming to have a specialty. You could pay her to do her specialty, but the more economical thing to do was to purchase a five-act performance, engaging all the women for seventy-five euros, and I lucked out when a group of Brits, just as I arrived, bought their pal Alan the package deal, since it was his fiftieth birthday.

Act One was that Alan got to massage this black lady, rubbing moisturizer all over her body—ass, legs, and breasts.

He was a blue-collar-looking fellow with cropped hair and gnarled hands, and he was rather drunk and I wondered if he had a wife back in England.

Act Two was a dark-haired white woman who put whipped cream on her nipples and Alan was allowed to suck the cream off, and then she put whipped cream on her shaved groin and he lapped that up.

The next gal, a blonde—Act Three—put a dildo in her pussy and then she had Alan stand back from the bar and she shot the dildo out of her pussy and hit him in the chest. He picked up the dildo off the floor and handed it back to her. She dipped it in a bucket of water to clean it and then she reloaded the dildo and shot him again, and this happened several times while his friends cheered and laughed. It reminded me of this game we used to play in high school where we kicked little paper footballs at each other across the cafeteria lunch tables. Then she had Alan climb up on the stage and she put the dildo in his zipper and held it there, and then she had him mount her and they sort of copulated, with the dildo acting as his penis. When he got off her, she grabbed the eyeglasses of one of his friends, a short little intoxicated man wearing a foolish red fez hat. She rubbed the spectacles on her pussy and then put the smeared lenses back on the fellow, who smiled happily.

Then came Act Four—the banana, the pièce de résistance. A nice Asian woman put a condom on a banana, for sanitary reasons I guess, and began to insert the banana in herself from various positions, giving a whole new meaning to the phrase "banana split." Then she lay back on the bar, holding on to the banana with her vagina, so that it stuck out of her, and rolled down the loose end of the condom and peeled the banana about halfway. This done, she took a knife and with a quick flick of her wrist, like a Jewish mohel, she sculpted a penile head on the banana. Then she put a dollop of whipped cream on the head of the banana/penis (ostensibly come or pre-come) and made Alan give her a blow job, which he did, and then made him eat the banana out of her pussy, which he also did. This homoerotic twist of him playing a fruit while eating a fruit was rather ingenious.

Act Five was another Asian woman, who was a little younger than the rest, maybe in her late twenties, and she squatted over the bar, put a pen in her vagina, and then placed a postcard—with a picture of the Banana Bar—beneath herself on a block of wood. Then with her vagina and a slight sway of her hips, she wrote, "Happy Birthday Alan." I leaned in and was quite impressed with the girl's penmanship.

After that I stepped away from the bar and saw the man in the fez hat take off his glasses, sniff them for a second to amuse one of his pals, and then clean them on his shirt, an action he had clearly performed thousands of times.

November 10

The next morning I woke up quite early: I had a train to catch to Berlin. I went to the bathroom to wash up and saw that my right nostril had doubled in size, that there was a small red marble under the skin. Back in the States I had been viciously picking my nose during a bad stretch of low funds—whenever I'm broke, I get nervous and I scratch my ass and pick my nose more than ever—and I had infected my nostril, probably from picking my nose with a dirty finger.

I thought, though, that the nostril-problem had more or less cleared up before the trip, but now it was back and the marble was pushing out of the nostril whereas before it had just been inside the nostril! My bad-mouthing of Danieleski the night before had already borne fruit! Karma! This was terrible. How could I go to Germany on a book tour with such a thing on my nose? On my Jewish nose! The Germans would kill me. They would have to change the tally: six million and one!

Naturally, I did the absolute wrong thing—I tried squeezing the pimple, and it increased in size by 25 percent. I wondered if I should cancel my trip to Germany.

But I knew that was ridiculous, and told myself to rely on one of the basic truths of human nature, which is that people are too self-involved to really look at each other, that no one would notice my nostril, that, in fact, only idiots like me perceive Ping-Pong balls on foreheads.

So I went to the station and Sedaris and Hugh were boarding a train to Paris. What happened next was sort of like the flashback scene in *Casablanca*, but a deeply neurotic *Casablanca*. I called out to them over the noises of the station: "David, Hugh!" They paused in the door, smiled in recognition, and waved. I continued: "I'm sorry for what I said about Danieleski's forehead! David, you're right. It probably was just a bruise![8] Now my nose has erupted. It's karma. I shouldn't have been so

[8] A few years later, I was speaking to a friend of Mark Danieleski's. It was reported to me that Danieleski had been told that I wrote about his lump in this essay, which originally appeared in the *New York Press*. Rather than be offended, Danieleski went to a doctor and was told that his growth, which he himself had somehow not been aware of, was a benign deposit of some sort. Turns out he was grateful that I had called his attention to something which could have been a tumor. So I guess my karma worked itself out.

rude. And now I'm going on a book tour in Germany with a gigantic pimple on my nose! I don't know if I can handle this!"

They just looked at me with slightly bewildered faces. I don't think they could hear me properly, so they waved good-bye one last time and then disappeared into their Paris-bound train. I had wanted Sedaris to give me absolution. I was hoping with my spontaneous confession to undo my bad karma and maybe instantaneously and magically clear up my nostril, but he hadn't been able to hear me, and so I was left on the platform with my guilt and my enormous pimple.

I staggered off to a bench and looked at pigeons dallying suicidally on the tracks, and I thought of *Anna Karenina*. I didn't want to take my own life, but I was feeling quite melancholic—the pimple had me down and I'm naturally depressed, anyway. Once I got on the train to Berlin, I started scribbling in my notebook. Like most people, I only write in my journal when I'm very sad. I've been keeping a journal for nearly twenty years and there's not a single happy entry.

I was busy writing down my woes when the man sharing my car, a fifty-something gent who smelled strongly of onions, said to me, "Excuse me, I'm from Austria but I read many books in English. Are you a writer? I think I know you."

"Yes, I am a writer," I said. Could I have possibly been recognized in Europe on a train? This was too flattering.

"Are you Nick Hornby?"

"No," I said, somewhat taken aback. "I'm not Nick Hornby."

"Oh, I'm sorry," said the man. "I saw a picture of him on a book—*About a Boy*—and he looked like you and you were writing in your diary, so I thought . . ."

"I understand," I said, and then I went through my mental Rolodex of author photos and realized that Hornby is pale and bald and dissipated. Why couldn't I be mistaken for a famously good-looking author, like Paul Auster? Why did I have to face the truth?

"What's your name?" he then asked. "You've written books? Maybe I've read you."

"I've written a few books. My name is Jonathan Ames."

"I haven't heard of you," said the man, bluntly. "I've read Jonathan Franzen and Jonathan Lethem."

"They're very good writers," I said. I looked out the window and in my mind I begged the man to stop talking to me. I was sharing a compartment with the best-read Austrian in the world and he was tormenting me.

"I'll look for your books on the Internet," he said.

"Thank you," I said, and then I excused myself and went to the bathroom and stared at my pimple. I tried again to pop the thing and added another 10 percent to its girth.

November 11, 12, 13, 14, 15, 16

The remaining days of my trip are a bit of a blur. My pimple, like something out of Kafka, grew larger and larger, making it hard for me to think of anything else. I asked the German photographers, who took my picture for the literary pages of various newspapers, to shoot me from only one side, like I was Streisand.

I saw Chelsea Clinton making out with her boyfriend in a cafe in East Berlin—she must have been on break from studying at Oxford—and I could have invited her to one of my readings, but I was too embarrassed because of my nose. All in all, I gave three readings and apologized to the audience each time about my pimple. They were very forgiving, but many people did comment that it was an awfully strange pimple. Some people were suggesting that perhaps it was a cyst of some kind.

Well, it finally all came to a head, as it were. My German publisher, to save money, had me staying in the apartment of the German liaison to the American consulate in Berlin. My hostess was an elegant older woman and she felt terrible about my nostril. She was one of the people who thought it was a cyst and not a pimple; in her opinion it was too large to be a pimple. So my last night in Berlin, she gave me some hydrocortisone cream, which she had bought once in the States. I think she figured I needed an American product since I'm an American writer.

Before going to bed, I repaired to the bathroom with the cream and read that it was good for, among other things, "anal itch." Why had I never been told this? I felt like I had needlessly endured years of suffering, but I also felt less alone in the world—at least my condition had been acknowledged. It was something worthy of being talked about on the side of a cortisone-cream tube. I knew that other people scratched their ass, but I had thought it was a once-in-a-while thing for the general public, not a chronic condition like I had. But seeing "anal itch" on the side of the tube, I suddenly knew that there must be legions of people with my problem.

I wondered, though, if I used the cortisone if my ass would ever be able to heal the itching on its own. Why I was worried about this I don't know, since my ass had not been able to heal itself for a decade and a half. The thing is, though, I tend to be against all Western medicines and I wanted my ass to find its own way. A chiropractor once told me that the best pharmacy in the world is in our own body—that we should be able to heal ourselves of most ailments.

Then I remembered that Bernie Williams had a good season for the Yankees after two cortisone shots in his shoulder, so this made me feel all right about cortisone—my love of baseball, and Bernie Williams in particular, had trumped my prejudice against Western medicine—and I applied some of the cream to my ass, and then put some on my ridiculous nose and went to sleep.

Well, in the middle of the night that cream did something to me. It was like my nostril had a wet dream. I sensed something and woke up. I put the light on and looked at myself in the mirror, which was on the closet next to the bed, and white fluid was dripping from my nose! I had abstained, like a good houseguest, from masturbating, but it had been to no avail. There was a wet spot on the pillow! I had soiled my German hostess's guest bed! It was either a cyst that was acting like a pimple or, quite simply, the largest pimple of my life had just turned my nostril into Pompeii. At the height of its maturity, the pimple had been the size of half a gumball.

I rushed to the bathroom, applied some hot water to my wound, and squeezed out some more white fluid, which is always one of life's great pleasures. The whole nose was inflamed, but there was hope—now that the white stuff was starting to come out, the thing would probably heal. I squeezed out more and felt a profound happiness, equal to what the Koan Float sensory deprivation tank had done for me. Who knew that squeezing a pimple was also a shortcut to Zen bliss.

So I'm pretty sure it wasn't a cyst, though not knowing how cysts behave or even what they look like, I can't say definitively. But for simplicity sake, I will maintain that it was a pimple and classify it as such. In fact, it was the grandest pimple ever. It had wrecked my European book tour!

By the time I returned to New York on November 17th, the nose, miraculously, was almost back to normal. I was now my regular ugly self, which I was grateful for. I had learned a valuable lesson: Appreciate the ugliness you do have, because it could get worse. And as an added benefit, my ass has stopped itching![9]

So all in all it was quite a good trip to Europe. I hope they publish more of my books—it's very self-improving to go over there.

2002

---

[9] The cortisone cream turned out to be a short-lived solution, but several people who read this essay when it was published in the *New York Press* took note of my itchy affliction and came forward with cures. I tried one of these cures, and if you want to find out if it worked—not that you should, since it's a rather disgusting topic—read the last essay of this collection.

Pleasant Bowel Syndrome (plez'ent bou'el sin'drom), n. A condition in which the body engages in the process of elimination without stress. In 2014, health nuts were finally able to convince the world that a vegetarian diet—rich with dark greens, fruits, whole grains, essential oils, and chocolate—was really the way to go, and so what was known as *irritable bowel syndrome* was eradicated. The conversion to a healthy diet meant that organic produce once more became the only kind of produce. The land was now properly tilled and not depleted of its nutrients. This proper use of land, led by a bunch of high-powered Whole Foods executives, led to the eradication of hunger throughout the world, and balance was restored: Sally Struthers slimmed down and numerous Africans began to put on weight. And of course, everyone was really happy now about going to the commode, and a lot of neurotic psychological bathroom hang-ups, which had been plaguing man for some time, were at last dropped, so to speak.

SNOWFALL

The recent heavy snow made me think of my friend Glen Seator, who is dead. In February of 1996 there was a bad snowfall, and Glen and I were very good friends back then.

I was living in Clinton Hill, Brooklyn, next to the BQE, and Glen was about two miles south of me, right next to the Manhattan Bridge. He lived on this weird little street—Duffield Street—of old houses which somehow had survived the building of both the BQE and the Manhattan Bridge.

Glen owned one of these old Duffield Street houses. He lived on the first floor and rented out the other two floors. It was a house he had bought with his longtime boyfriend back in the 1980s, but that relationship ended and Glen was left as the sole owner. He loved his building, but it was also, I think, a constant reminder of his heartbreak, of something lost.

So there was a blizzard this one day in February, and Glen called me up late in the afternoon as it was getting dark, as the storm came to an end, and asked if I could come over and help him shovel off his roof. The roof was going to collapse or leak, something like that.

I walked under the BQE to Glen's. Nothing had been plowed. I felt like an adventurer.

We went up to his roof. Glen was in his late thirties, tall, redheaded, handsome, and a little arrogant—but the kind of arrogant that is charming; it made people crave his approval, which is probably why I was on that roof. He was also terribly funny, a WASP from the Midwest who could do the best imitation of a yenta I have ever come across, and I should know, having grown up with yentas. Once this talent was revealed, we spent most of our time together talking in what we called "yenta," which meant that we harassed and insulted one another in our best yenta-Yiddish accents:

"You're horrible! You're selfish!" he'd cry.

"You're the one who's selfish!" I'd say. "I come to your home and you don't even think of offering me something to eat! I could starve to death and you wouldn't even notice!"

"I know better than to give you something to eat! You're a *shnorrer*! A pig! If I gave you a cracker you'd eat my whole freezer!"

So we were up there on the roof shoveling. The snow was wet and heavy. The sun went down. I was terribly cold. The roof was slippery and slanted. It seemed an impossible task. I kept hoping Glen would say we should quit, but with light coming from the high-powered lamps of the Manhattan Bridge, just enough light to see by, we somehow cleared that roof in about two hours—the white snow giving way to black tar.

Then Glen made me dinner. He was a wonderful cook. We spoke, as always, in yenta, which gave me great pleasure; I've rarely laughed with anyone as much as I laughed with Glen. After dinner, I walked back home under the cover of the BQE.

Over the next year or so we drifted apart. We talked less and less. He was often out of the country for weeks and months at a time. He was a genius artist: Museums all over the world solicited him for the architectural installations he would build. It's not easy to describe his work, but if I was to simplify things, I'd say that he took apart the museums and galleries that hired him in order to *expose* these institutions, or, conversely, he rebuilt their structures within their structures. I think his idea was to displace as well as to reveal. And once he said to me, describing his work, "I like to make a mess. It's a way to be bad."

This seemed fitting, because Glen's arrogance made him careless, distracted; he didn't like to be bothered with the annoying things one has to do, and so his affairs were always *a mess*—bills went unpaid, documents were lost, his building was always falling apart—and yet he managed to make breathtaking work that required precision and discipline, even as it disrupted. His art was a rebellion: *I'll play by the rules to show that I can't stand the rules.* So the results were displacing, revealing, and mess-making, but also beautiful.

These last few years, I didn't see him at all, except once by chance in a restaurant about two years ago. Seeing him I immediately missed him, and we said we'd get together, but we didn't.

Then a mutual friend, Ava, called me this winter, a few days after Christmas. She said, "I have something to tell you."

"Okay," I said, and I knew from her voice to gird myself for something terrible.

"I'm sorry to be the one with bad news, but I'm just going to say it. . . . Glen Seator died. He fell off his roof. He was up there fixing something and fell off. They found him the next day. Can you believe it?"

I couldn't believe it, and I still can't. I never fully believe that people die. Don't want to believe.

I told Ava—because I'm *self-centered, horrible*—that one time I had been on that roof with him and I found it slanted and dangerous. I told her this, I think, to show that I had once been good enough friends with him to have been up there shoveling in the freezing cold, and that I had intimate knowledge, in a way, of how and why he died. It was my ego asserting itself: I was there: We were good friends.

My ego did this to compensate for the fact that I hadn't really seen or spoken to him in years, that actually he had died for me while he had still been alive. Our friendship had died.

I don't have any photographs of Glen and I haven't cried over him, but if I had a picture I probably would cry—it would drive home to me that I'll never see him again; that there's no second chance of running into him at a restaurant and this time making a call. I've had other friends who've died and it's when I look at their photos that I want to scratch at the pictures and bring them back, bring them back as alive as they were in the moment the pictures were taken.

Ever since Ava gave me the news about Glen, I often morbidly wonder what he thought as he plummeted. I think he must not have believed that it was happening, he must not have thought he would die—he always seemed so sure of everything, so certain. Or maybe there was terror and horrible fear, the realization that he had made a grotesque mistake.

I'd like if it was the former, that he felt momentarily annoyed and inconvenienced, that he figured he'd be bruised, but all right. What I'd truly like, though, is to go by his house and see him, to knock on his door like I used to seven years ago and have him be there. He couldn't possibly have fallen off his roof. I don't really believe it.

2003

CLUB EXISTENTIAL DREAD

A men's *magazine sent me to a Club Med resort located in Turks and Caicos, a small chain of magnificent islands in the British West Indies. I went for a week. The magazine expected me to file a salacious report. The following diary is what I submitted. The magazine did not run it. Not salacious enough, I guess. Or, perhaps, it was salacious in the wrong ways. Who knows. Regardless, McSweeney's kindly ran the piece and so here it is:*

Day 1, July 2
8:33 A.M.

I'm on the plane, just after a shaky takeoff. Having my usual fears of dying. The seats of the plane are old, like 1970s furniture, which is not very reassuring. Other than dying, my chief concern is how I will get sunblock on my back, which, I guess, is dying-related.

1:34 P.M.

Unpacked and in my room. Will go to the beach. The ocean, an uncanny blue, like Peter O'Toole's eyes in *Lawrence of Arabia*, is quite beautiful. The compound is essentially a festive college dormitory but with a beach, outdoor bar, and pool.

Nearly had trouble at the airport. The passport guy asked me why my eyes were yellow. I noticed a poster warning about SARS. I said, "They get that way when I'm tired." He studied my passport some more. Then he said he'd be right back. I was worried that he thought I was a drug addict with hepatitis and wasn't going to let me in.

I didn't want to explain that I have Gilbert's syndrome; I thought it would sound too ludicrous, but I didn't think he'd leave his station to consult with superiors. . . . He was gone almost five minutes. The whole line was stalled. This was serious. I had a stupid smile on my face when he came back, which is not the kind of face to have around passport guys, makes you look nervous and guilty. He said, "Can you tell me again why your eyes are yellow?"

"I have Gilbert's syndrome," I said. "It's a benign genetic condition; I'm missing an enzyme in my liver and when I'm tired, my eyes get yellow."

I was telling him the truth but I felt like I was lying. Who speaks of liver enzymes to passport control guys?

"Oh, all right," he said, and stamped my passport. "I thought maybe you had yellow fever."

So he let me into his country to spread Gilbert's syndrome, which I guess I could do if I get someone pregnant and pass on the necessary flawed gene to the child.

11:15 P.M.

Spoke to a petite, pretty Sri Lankan woman from L.A. before dinner. She invited me to sit with her by the bar. I asked
her what she thought of the place.

"If you want to get laid," she said, "this is the place. If
that's what you're looking for. I'm not. I'm here to scuba. Also,
it was cheap. Chicks fly free to Club Med."

"Really?"

"Yeah, that's why I came. A free ticket is too good to pass
up. . . . It's my last night tonight, so maybe I will kiss a cute
boy."

I wondered if this excluded me. Probably. I'm pale and bald
and the rings under my eyes are so deep they reach the back of
my head. Anyway, I can't do any kissing. I have a girlfriend and
I'm off booze. Who comes to Club Med under these condi-
tions? No one. I shouldn't have accepted this assignment.

I left the Sri Lankan and went in to dinner. I sat with a
group of twenty-somethings. Conversation was dull and in-
nocuous. One guy has second-degree burns on his feet and is
walking around in socks filled with aloe. I must avoid his fate
and be diligent with my sunblock.

After dinner, they had what's called a "Foam Party."
They fenced off a little area by the pool, about the size of a
squash court, and set up some kind of Willy Wonka machine
which emitted huge gushes of foam—soap bubbles and maybe
sperm from the male staff. The idea was for people to dance
in the foam-sperm.

I took off my shirt and went in. At the entrance, the foam
came up to my stomach. My shorts got damp. Girls were in

bikinis. They were all wiggling about to the music. The occasional bikini bottom rubbed against me, lubricated with wet foam.

To get the full experience, I thought I should go to the source of the foam—a big drainage pipe propped up on a ladder—and stand beneath it. So I did. Here the foam was up to my shoulders. There were about a hundred of us packed into the pit.

Then a new gush of foam was ejaculated. The foam poured over my head.

I couldn't breathe.

I couldn't see.

I sucked foam into my lungs.

I made a panicked, forceful push to get out of there, like someone trying to escape a burning nightclub. It was hard going. I was blind.

I really felt like I was going to die.

I was drowning on soap bubbles and staff-sperm.

Somehow I got out of the pit. An hour later, I'm still coughing up soap.

Day 2, July 3
1:05 P.M.

On a quiet beautiful beach, under an umbrella. One beach is noisy; this one is quiet.

About ten yards away is an attractive topless woman. I was ashamed but when she walked by I asked her if she could put sunblock on the middle of my back. She's Jewish. A fellow Jew. I noticed the "Chai" on her necklace. I thought of saying, "Chai," instead of "Hi," which would be a good opening line with a Jewish girl.

From yesterday, I have a burn spot in the middle of my back the size of a serving tray. I can reach the tops of my shoulders and my lower back, but not my middle.

She rubbed the lotion on; it was rather sensual, but then she said, dismissively, reading the label, "Fifty?"

"I'm very fair," I said, like a milquetoast, which I literally am: a white piece of toast.

I figure I need fifty. In one minute I would fry, so fifty gives me fifty minutes without frying. I wish there were an invention that would enable shy people to put sunblock on their back by themselves. A spatula would work, and the association with frying is apt.

This place should be called Club High School. The cool people, with their beautiful bodies and tans and a large capacity for liquor, hang out at the noisy beach and the pool.

I'm some kind of artist-snob. I'm ugly and poor but snobby. Everyone here seems so bourgeois. They're burghers. I wonder if that word is related to bourgeois. Or rather they're like burgers—human burgers frying themselves in the sun. If a bunch of dermatologists came here they'd be hysterical, they'd lose their minds.

Bourgeois. Burghers. Burgers.

Last night I was woken up at 4:50 A.M. by shouts of "One more!" and "Take it off!" My room was next to the after-hours bar, Sharkies. I went to see what was happening. Five girls were lying on the bar, all in a row, like slaughtered fish. They all looked like Monica Lewinsky—chubby but with nice faces. The bartender was pouring vodka down their throats from a bottle with a spigot. I was worried the girls could die from alcohol poisoning.

Guys with cancerous tans and dyed blond hair were urging the girls to take off their tops. Several of the girls did expose their bras. But none of them flashed any boobs. I staggered back to my room.

This morning I asked to be shifted to the other side of the compound.

11:30 P.M.

I have a doppelgänger here. There's a weird lonely guy whose nose is attached in a strange way to his lip, like a bird. He wears a baseball hat, is bald underneath, and is completely white. He was wearing sneakers and socks on the beach. He hovers around the edges of things and talks to no one. I should talk to him. Be friendly. I should talk to all the lonely ones. But I can't.

Day 3, July 4, Independence Day
10 A.M.

I went to the nurse and asked her to put sunblock on my back. She's in her fifties, blonde, and covered in cancer-freckles. She applied my sunblock with a rubber glove. My own sense of germ-propriety agreed with her use of the rubber glove. Also, the humiliation of it appealed to me masochistically. Confirmed my utter loser status here.

1:40 P.M.

To celebrate the 4th, they released all these red, white, and blue soy balloons, which are environmentally safe. Vegetarian seagulls can eat them. The balloons looked beautiful in the sky, like a gigantic DNA helix.

7 P.M.

My body is completely falling apart. I was at the beach and felt this lump on the back of my head. I decided to squeeze it. A clear fluid, like baby oil, came out. The lump was reduced in size by about 60 percent. What the hell was that oil? Was the thing a zit or a cyst? Probably a combination. A zyst.

Then my crotch began to hurt. I have massive weltish jock itch from sitting in a wet bathing suit for three days. Luckily, I packed fungus cream for the preexisting jock itch I have in my ass. But I'm almost out of the stuff. I will have to ration it between my ass and my crotch. I don't know how much more pathetic I can become.

At five-thirty, there was a softball game. I watched it briefly. My doppelgänger was playing. He was actually picked last. Then he nearly struck out. With two strikes, he hit a weak grounder to first and ran heroically but didn't make it. At least he hit the ball. If he had struck out, I might have had to kill myself.

12:30 A.M.

I've been watching a *Twilight Zone* marathon. There was an episode where a beautiful woman lived in a world of ugly people and so she was considered hideous. That's kind of like me and the doppelgänger. Except we really are ugly.

Day 4, July 5
11:36 A.M.

Went to the nurse again this morning, but there was a young, pretty one today. She said: "You are very white."

This wounded me a little; I thought I had some color. I've gone from alabaster to pale.

She didn't wear a rubber glove, which is nice, made me feel quasi-human.

10:30 P.M.

The place is putting its spell on me. Despite my best intentions I feel happy. Sat on the beach and read. Kept thinking the insipid banal thought, This is the life.

Then I went snorkeling. On the boat to the reef, I met a lively cute girl, K., a brunette with a nice figure. She put sunblock on my back. Not a nurse! She said, "I love the smell of this stuff."

"It smells like a Creamsicle," I said.

"I want to eat your sunblock," K. said.

She asked me to be her snorkeling partner. Her crotch, underwater, as I swam behind her, was very appealing—the necessary and lovely parting of her legs.

I spotted an enormous stingray and two six-foot nurse-sharks. Supposedly they don't attack. It was scary, but K. was intrepid, following them, so I had to as well.

I had dinner with K. and her friends. They told me that everyone was fucking on the beach at night. Then K. told me about this girl who was sharing a room with another girl—

this girl didn't come with a friend and they housed her with a stranger. To save money, some people share rooms. So every night this girl could hear her roommate masturbating.

I said to K., "What did the girl say it sounded like? There was moaning?"

"I asked the same question," K. said. "She wasn't moaning. The girl said it sounded like this. . . ." And with that K. took her lower lip, pinched it, and shook it back and forth, re-creating the sound of a clit being stroked rapidly. All the girls laughed.

After dinner, like every night, there was entertainment. Tonight there was a sweet competition between four couples to elect the best couple of Club Med, like King and Queen of the prom, continuing the theme of *This Is High School.* But everything is high school. Maybe everything is just life and high school was a part of life. A couple from my home state of New Jersey won, which made me proud. There's a few people here from New Jersey. Most of the people are from Canada, New York, and L.A. Three countries.

I'm watching a *Planet of the Apes* marathon.

I'm going to call P. Been missing her. Looking forward to talking to her.

Day 5, July 6
11:30 A.M.

Had a terrible phone call with P. last night. A fight. It lasted an hour. She's upset that I'm at Club Med. Feel all hungover from the fight. God only knows how much that phone call will cost.

K. and her friends left today, and the doppelgänger left. All my friends are gone.

Day 6, July 7
11:30 P.M.

Had a deep-tissue massage on the dock by the water. A lot of unhappiness and stress was released. I kept crying out in pain. I screamed: "I confess!" The sweet female masseuse laughed.

All day I swam, the light shining in the water like sequins.

They're really converting me. The yellow has drained from my eyes. I feel healthy.

The Club Med ethos *is* a bit forced: the staff shouting at us all the time to make noise, to clap, to be happy. It's summer camp for adults. But it sort of works. If you act happy, your brain starts to believe you're happy.

Day 7, July 8
3:30 P.M.

I'm in the airport, waiting to go. All I did yesterday was swim and read. Quite blissful.

Got the bill. That phone call cost $150. Oh, well. It will be good to see P., to not be alone.

In the van here to the airport, I was with three very pretty women. As we left Club Med, all these people were there saying good-bye to the women, crying. No one was there to say good-bye to me. Hardly anyone knew I was there for a week. Except the nurses. It reminds me of summer camp when I was thirteen. On the last day, everybody was weeping, parting from their friends. I had made no friends. So I took a picture of two beautiful girls to show my parents, to pretend that I had made friends. It depresses me to remember this.

But I'm making progress in life. When we got to the airport, I helped the women with their enormous bags and they were very grateful and friendly. And then just a few minutes ago I spoke to this one woman from the van, here in the waiting area, and she was intrigued to learn that I had come to Club Med to write about it, and then she wrote down the titles of my books. This other woman from the van started listening in and they both acted like they wished they had met me sooner. So I guess I'm not without some charm! And the real sign of growth since summer camp long ago is that I have no intention of asking them if I can take their picture.

2003

My great-aunt, Doris, July 13, 2003.

THE MOST PHALLIC
BUILDING IN THE WORLD:
A FIVE-DAY DIARY FOR *SLATE*

July 14—You Spent Money!

Today is Monday, but I'll tell you what I did yesterday, Sunday.

Every other Sunday, just about, I go visit my great-aunt Doris. She turned ninety-one in February.

Yesterday followed the standard routine: I picked up a *New York Post* and a coffee, and scandalized myself with the paper during the rather long subway ride from my Brooklyn neighborhood to her Queens neighborhood—twenty-four stops, about fifty minutes.

At the station in Queens there is a florist who operates out of a narrow little space but has beautiful flowers, and I always try to choose an interesting arrangement. Over the years, the florist, a sweet, gentle bear of a man, has come to know me and often gives me a free flower or two. Yesterday, I picked camellias, yellow daisies, two white-orange roses, and a sunflower, and the florist gave me a pink carnation.

Then I went to Ben's Best Deli to pick up lunch. One of the men behind the counter—I think he's Russian—has also come to know me and always says in his accent: "How are you today, young man?" A few years ago, he asked me: "Excuse me for asking. But I see you for a long time with flowers. You go to your girlfriend?"

When I told him whom I visited, he smiled broadly, and after that he's always greeted me so sweetly and usually gives me a piece of hot corned beef right from his hand. Because it's from him, I don't worry about germs. He and the florist are both very kind to me. Yesterday, the deli man wasn't behind the counter, and I missed him.

I went to my great-aunt's building and she opened her apartment door and gave me a joyous smile; we are like Kabuki actors—we do the same thing every time. After the smile, she admonished me and said, indicating the flowers, "You spent money!" She always says it with great sincerity, but then lovingly puts the flowers in a vase on the windowsill and cares for them in the days that follow, trying to make them last as long as she can. She hardly ever leaves the apartment and sees almost no one.

After I hugged her to my chest and kissed the top of her head—she's very tiny, like a child—we ate the lunch I brought. Then I lay on her couch and read her *People* magazine, a guilty pleasure, and she read the *Post*. Then I convinced her to go for a walk. We passed an old man, and she said, "A man who lives alone can go to a bar at midnight if he's lonesome and talk to

the bartender. But if I did that they'd think I was a pickup."
She often tells me this, explaining why she has few options for
her loneliness. Then we came back and played gin rummy.

After about four hours I had to leave and said, "I love you,"
and she said, "I love you more than that," and when I was on
the street I looked up at her window and could see the flowers.

July 15—Hold Your Papers!

Yesterday was Bastille Day. But I didn't do anything French.
Well, maybe one thing, but I'll get to that.

So what *did* I do yesterday? How Proustian—a fitting
allusion for Bastille Day—can I be in my recall? Of course, I
haven't actually read Proust. Or Freud. Or Jung. Or Marx.
Or Darwin. And yet I inform my worldview with ideas from
all these men. When I try to remember things, I think of
Proust. When I get annoyed with my father, I think of Freud.
When I think that another human being—a female—will
complete me, I think of Jung. When I think of the soul-
crushing ennui of most jobs, I think of Marx. When I try to
understand why I'm bald, I think of Darwin.

I have an idea of their notions from what I've picked up
in the culture, but I'm sure that I've got everything all wrong.
I've played the intellectual version of the telephone game: I've
received their theories completely distilled and distorted. No
wonder I'm screwed up. My whole philosophical foundation is
based on rumor, innuendo, and insinuation, not to mention
hearsay.

I do take consolation in the undistilled words of one great
thinker, Neil Young: "Though my problems are meaningless

that don't make them go away." So I have no idea what's going on, my worldview is completely flawed, and my life is meaningless, but it doesn't go away and here's a slice of it, my Bastille Day 2003:

(1) Woke up at 6:30, after a night of lurid, violent dreams, to write yesterday's diary entry by deadline. Finished at 9. Staggered about the apartment for a few hours.

(2) At 1 P.M. went out to buy fruit, thinking that I needed more fruit in my life. Purchased grapefruits, mangoes, blueberries, and plums.

(3) Stopped at my favorite bookstore, Bookcourt, and was stunned anew by the sheer number of books. It looked like there were more books than human beings and I wondered if the publishing industry wasn't some kind of money-laundering scam.

(4) Stopped at my coffee place. The coffee is expensive but they always have a *New York Times* lying about, and so that evens things out nicely. My whole adult life I've been trying to get free newspapers. In the early nineties, I used to drive a taxi in Princeton, New Jersey. Across from the taxi stand was a Burger King that opened at 6 A.M. Around 8 A.M., I'd go in there and make a sweep of the papers: *Trenton Times, Trentonian, Newark Star-Ledger,* and the three NYC papers. All these old-timers would be in there. They gathered every morning to study the horse races before going to OTB. I'd come through, grabbing papers, and this one ancient fellow, the group's leader, would say to his comrades: "Hold your papers, hold your papers, here he comes." That senior citizen and I did battle for several years.

(5) After coffee, worked for about two hours on this article I'm writing for a men's magazine. The magazine sent me

to Club Med for a week in the Caribbean, a sweet gig, but I'm off booze and in a relationship. I don't think they knew this when they gave me the assignment. I think they're expecting a scandalous tale of alcohol and sex. I hope they don't make me pay them back for the trip.

(6) In the late afternoon, my girlfriend and I lay down for a nap. At some point the nap turned rigorous, and I'm not yet forty, but I had an understanding of how men could have heart attacks while exerting themselves romantically. I think I made more of an effort than usual and the old heart could have easily exploded like a cheap balloon.

(7) Went to the gym for twenty minutes to work on preventing heart attacks. An attractive woman lay next to me on the stretching mat and she assumed the missionary position and began thrusting her hips into the air. I considered the wisdom of the Muslim approach to separating the sexes.

(8) Had dinner with my girlfriend and my friend David Leslie, who told us of his plans to become a professional boxer. He's forty-five and has been having a midlife crisis for some time now. He and I had a boxing match three years ago in front of six hundred spectators and he beat me up nicely. Broke my nose, dislocated my jaw, and gave me a concussion. This was done in the name of performance art. I also bloodied his nose and landed many stiff jabs, but he had twenty-five pounds on me and used some dirty tactics. Somehow we're still friends.

(9) My girlfriend and I watched Bergman's *The Seventh Seal*. Young Max von Sydow's face was incredible to look at. Luminous and deathly. At the end of the film, the knight dies and the fool lives. That's the kind of story I like.

July 16—Doggy Style!

I started out yesterday rather happy and blithe, and for many hours was oozing joie de vivre, but by the end of the day I was feeling rather blacklungish with fear.

Let me try to trace what happened, perhaps to understand why I lost my sense of well-being, which was so nice while it lasted.

Woke up early, 6:50, to write my diary. Drank coffee, which went directly to my writing gland, and by 10, I had typed out the thing. All was well.

At 10:30, I did a phone interview with a radio station in Canada. I was being interviewed to promote my appearance at the Montreal Comedy Festival, July 17–18. I'm part of something called "Reading It," where a few of us writers will read what we hope are humorous pieces, especially since it's a comedy festival.

Like Jack Benny, but in a literary way, I often do the same routine now whenever I give readings. I have two essays from my book *What's Not to Love?* that are always crowd-pleasers and I recite them repeatedly. Their titles are self-explanatory: "Bald, Impotent, and Depressed," and "I Shit My Pants in the South of France."

Since I'll be in Montreal, I'll probably read my Francophile essay. Before doing so, I'll make my usual apology, which goes like this: "I've come to notice that the world is divided between those who like scatological humor and those who don't. For those of you who don't, please try to see my story as a classic tale of hubris, of excessive pride."

I have to say, ever since I penned that South of France piece, I've received the most incredible confessions from people about their bowels. One man told me of heroically getting to a restaurant toilet in time, but then exploding before he could get his pants off. We all know that moment of terror, but most of us survive. This guy didn't. Well, the poor fellow wanted to take off his pants and try to clean himself up, but he was idiotically wearing military boots and had managed to knot the laces and couldn't pull his pants over his shoes! He was stuck in the stall and had to ask another person in the bathroom to get him a steak knife so he could cut through his laces.

Anyway, I did the radio interview, and for the next several hours I didn't have a care in the world. I wasn't nervous at all. I'm practically broke, surviving off credit cards, which is always upsetting, but yesterday it didn't bother me at all. I was at peace.

I did try to work on my novel, which is about an alcoholic with a nose fetish, but I was in too good a mood to concentrate. Then somehow it was six o'clock, and I hadn't done a thing and a nervous thought penetrated my mild euphoria: What will I write for tomorrow's diary entry? I came up with a plan—walk across the Brooklyn Bridge, and then go see *Terminator 3*. I figured that would make a good installment.

I headed for the bridge. I kept meeting dogs along the way. Whenever I go for walks, I troll for love from anonymous dogs. First, I ask the human owner if I can pet their dog. Then I get down on my knees and the dogs love me up and lick the wax out of my ears. I nuzzle their necks and practically give them a hickey. What I'd really love to do is to lie on a field with a hundred dogs and just roll around and have an orgy of affection. I'd prefer that to a human orgy.

Well, I made love—in the old-fashioned sense—to several dogs yesterday, and by the time I got to the bridge, I had lost interest in crossing it. So I went to this park beneath the bridge and met some more dogs.

Then I went to see *Terminator*. I like going to movies by myself. I loudly guffaw, chuckle, chortle, and emote. After *Terminator*, which I enjoyed in a sort of lobotomized way with occasional vocal outbursts, I snuck into the Johnny Depp pirate movie. It was during this enjoyable film that I began to crash emotionally. It may have only been low blood sugar—I hadn't eaten for hours—but suddenly I felt very sad. I thought of my parents. Lately, I haven't been very generous with them on the phone, hurrying off, and the shortness of life struck me—who am I to hurry off the phone? We don't live forever. I have to love my parents *now* before it's too late. Then I had a delayed reaction to the apocalyptic crap of *Terminator*. So many movies are about the end of the world, and I worry about some kind of mad subconscious universal wish fulfillment being channeled through Hollywood.

By the time I limped home after midnight, I was done for, and it has kind of carried over to today. But it's ten o'clock now and I know what to do. I'm going to call my parents and talk until *they* want to hang up, and then I'm going for a walk to look for some dogs to love.

July 17—The Most Phallic Building in the World!

Yesterday, my girlfriend and I went to Coney Island. It was overcast, the sky looked like it was pregnant with skim milk, but we were feeling intrepid and so we went anyway.

I always like the subway ride to Coney Island, because the train comes out of its hole beneath the ground, like a worm trying something new, and flies above the borough for most of the journey. It becomes an *elevated* train, though it doesn't act pretentious.

When it first pops out of the ground, you can see, on your right, the ocean and the Marlon Brandoish docks; on the left, you can see, dominating the Brooklyn skyline, the Williamsburgh Bank Building, which is the most obviously phallic building I've ever seen. It's so penislike it's embarrassing. Some clever lesbian gal in Park Slope—a Brooklyn neighborhood with a healthy Sapphic population—should design a Williamsburgh Bank dildo, market it over the Web, and make a fortune, since all New York–themed trinkets are in demand.

I have to say, the eye is always drawn to this bank-penis. Living in Brooklyn is like being in a locker room with Shaquille O'Neal. You can't help but stare.

Anyway, we took the wormlike subway to Avenue X— a very cool name for an avenue—where we had to transfer to a bus. And it's fitting that I should have just used the word "worm" to describe the subway, because on the bus was this wonderful gal named Angelica, whom I once witnessed eating worms at the Coney Island Freak Show.

She's a very pretty young lady who, in addition to having a courageous palate, is heavily tattooed. She's also well-pierced. Her face and nose have numerous silver studs, and her eyebrows have been shaved and replaced with a row of holes that must house piercings, though yesterday these holes were empty.

When we got off the bus, I introduced myself and my girlfriend to Angelica, and we told her that we had seen her show a few months ago. She was exceedingly friendly and sweet, and allowed me to take her picture. I complimented her on the worm business, and she said, with some embarrassment, that that's what she does for "family shows," but for adult shows, she can be more outrageous. "I do fire tricks," she said. "I shoot fire from my crotch. You can't do that in a family show."

She also performs in a burlesque on Friday nights. "I'm in a straitjacket," she said, describing her act, "and as I struggle to get out of it, my skirt comes off, then my bra. And then everything is off, except for the pasties and a G-string."

I know quite a few girls in the burlesque world, and coming up with new ways to strip is not easy, and so I really admired the sound of this straitjacket routine.

We then said good-bye to Angelica and made our way to the boardwalk. We strolled from Coney Island to Brighton Beach, which is about a fifteen-minute walk. The whole Brooklyn coast is beautiful, but something has gone wrong in New York. Coney Island/Brighton Beach really should be our Santa Monica or Rio or Miami. Instead it's rather worn out and tired, though it's also undeniably charming; it has the beauty of lost grandeur.

On the boardwalk in Brighton Beach, we went to a Russian restaurant, which is like saying we went to a Chinese restaurant in Chinatown. Brighton Beach is more Russian than American, which is wonderful. For the price of a subway ride, you can go to a foreign country.

At Tatiana, the menu was in English and Russian, though in the past in Brighton Beach I've sometimes been mistaken for a Russian and been given menus that don't have any English. But the waiter pegged my girlfriend and me as tourists, so we got the bilingual bill of fare. All around us people were speaking the language of Tolstoy, and on the boardwalk, ancient Russians staggered by, as if Tarkovsky had filmed *The Night of the Living Dead.*

We ordered the smoked fish plate and fried potatoes. The food was delicious and plentiful. The fish plate had two eggs with salmon caviar and four pieces each of salmon, sturgeon, butterfish, and something called *semga.* When the waiter served us, I said to him, "What kind of fish is 'smegma'?" I hadn't intended to be vulgar, but it came out that way, a kind of momentary Tourette's. Luckily, he didn't understand me; his English was limited. We never found out what *semga* is, but it looks like char.

After our feast, we went into the ocean. We didn't bring our bathing suits because of the overcast sky, but now it was sunny out. I swam in my boxer shorts and my girlfriend wore her panties and bra. We felt self-conscious, but, of course, nobody looked at us. The water was delightful.

We dried off with a windbreaker I had in my backpack. Then I wrapped my jacket around my waist and slipped off my wet underwear and pulled on my dry shorts. I nearly exposed my own little Williamsburgh Bank when the jacket slipped, but disaster was averted. Not that anybody would have noticed. I'm no Shaquille O'Neal, if you know what I mean.

July 18—This American Erection!

Yesterday, my penis nearly exploded when I flew to Montreal. I hate when that happens.

On the plane, I sat next to an ancient fellow with a raggedy gray beard and a tragic face. He bore a resemblance to some inner notion I have of Don Quixote and he was reading Joyce's *Portrait of the Artist as a Young Man*. I was pleased to see someone indulging in literature, but couldn't think of an opening salvo of dialogue to engage him. None of these lines, which I considered, would have worked:

"You haven't read it before?" (This was too rude, implying that he was old.)

"What do you think of it?" (Joyce doesn't really lend itself to an airplane discussion.)

"Are you, by any chance, in a production of *Man of La Mancha*?" (Also too rude.)

So I didn't bug the fellow and shortly after takeoff I passed out, which often happens to me on planes. The stress of the whole ordeal acts as a sedative. First there's the trauma of getting to the airport, and then there's the overload of guilt feelings I experience as I pass through security. You see, when I go through the metal detectors, I think I should be stopped and arrested; beaten and lashed would also work. I'm not carrying any weapons, but I feel like a bad person. I feel like that all the time, but I'm most conscious of it at checkpoints with authority figures.

I once read a self-help book in the eighties—I don't remember the title, it was something like "All Families Are Sick"—and the author addressed the reader at one point and said: "You think you are bad and deserve to be punished." That's me! Yet somehow I escape punishment at airports. But the life of a fugitive, I find, is exhausting, and so I pass out soon after I'm seated on a plane.

When I woke up halfway through the short flight to Montreal, I discovered that the comely stewardess had put an immigration card on my lap, which was forward of her in a pleasant way. I took a pen out of my jacket pocket and dispatched with the form. I went to put the pen back, but then I remembered that my pens often erupt when I fly, and over the years I've destroyed several shirts and one sport coat. Yesterday, I was wearing my prized seersucker jacket and certainly didn't want a pen to explode in its beautiful confines. I needed the jacket to be in good shape for my performances here at the *Juste Pour Rire* comedy festival. So, feeling very clever, I put the pen in my backpack. Sometimes I do learn from past errors.

Shortly thereafter, the plane landed. I was sitting next to the window. My seatmate with the mournful countenance got up first, and I followed close behind. Too close behind, literally: My foot snagged on something and I bumped into Don Quixote's rear quarter. This might not have been so bad, except the air pressure which causes pens to explode had caused my penis to swell impressively, and the thing jabbed into the ancient Joyce fan like a shiv in a prison fight or something else that people jab into others in prisons, the something else that it was. I don't think he was aware of what had stabbed him, he just looked over his shoulder with a questioning look as I dismounted from him like a stallion from a mare. We exchanged our first and only line of dialogue. "Sorry," I said. He nodded and proceeded up the aisle.

I also proceeded up the aisle, and my erection wouldn't go down. I covered it with the flap of my seersucker. The thing was really protruding. I recalled that this had happened to me before on planes, but I couldn't put my penis in my backpack as I had my pen.

I got out of the plane, and up ahead was a fellow performer in the festival whom I had been chatting with in the airport lounge—Sarah Vowell, a fine writer of several books and an editor for the wildly popular radio program *This American Life*. She's a very attractive young woman, with a proper and civilized demeanor, and I didn't want her to see that I was having priapic airsickness. Luckily, she didn't wait for me, but I knew I'd catch up to her at passport control. So as I walked through the airport, I tried to do yoga breaths to bring the thing down. But I wear boxer shorts and I think the lack of restriction was working against me. As I walked I jiggled and my penis misread this as encouragement to keep it up, so to speak. Ahead of me I could see Sarah. I'll never get on NPR, I wailed in my mind. Forget about *This American Life*, Ames, I told myself, this American Erection in Canada is going to be your undoing. Maybe I can be on *This American Death*.

I approached passport control and was still ready to star in a porn film, but then I was handed a SARS form. I thought of answering yes to all the questions—Do you have a fever? Have you French-kissed a SARS-affected person?—so that I could be taken to a back room and given a cold shower. Don't they throw cold water on prisoners to make them speak? But then for some reason, my erection went down. I think reading about SARS did it.

I caught up to Sarah and we traveled together to the hotel and performed on the same bill last night. All is well. NPR, here I come! So to speak.

2003

Pro-Semitism (pro-sem'it'is'um), n. A state of mind in which a person feels positively about Jews. Before 2018, there was a word known as *anti-Semitism,* which essentially described a mind-set where a person was hostile toward Jews and found them annoying, to say the least. But all this started to change in 2005 when an Israeli boy was playing on one side of a fence and a Palestinian boy was playing on the other side and the two started talking in English, which in 2005 had become the Universal Second Language. They started rolling small Hot Wheels cars back and forth to each other through holes in the fence and while they played, they complained about their parents. "My mother won't let me eat bacon," said the Jewish boy. "I'd really like to try it." "That's weird," said the Palestinian boy. "My mother won't let me eat bacon either!" Well, those two boys realized that they had a lot in common and grew up to be great friends and eventually, in 2018, they became the leaders of their people. United by a desire to try bacon at least once, plus the realization that their two clans had a great deal in common, these two leaders hired the world's greatest genealogist, Olaf Grtznjkg, from the historically neu-tral country of Iceland, and this genealogist discovered that all Palestinians and Israelis were actually third cousins. Now, this might not sound like a profound connection, but for Jewish and Muslim people family is very important. Certain retired Jewish people in Florida have been known to go to great lengths to find fourth cousins to send joke e-mails to. Anyway, once it was discovered that Palestinians and Israelis were cousins, relations between those people became absolutely joyous. Their happiness at realizing they didn't have to fight anymore was wonderfully infectious and spread throughout the whole world. The two states, Palestine and Israel, started to live side by side, and they were as happy together as Connecticut and Massachusetts. The Palestinians let everyone know that Jews were okay and that they had a wonderful sense of humor. The films of Woody Allen began to be broadcast on the Al-Jazeera network; Egyptians, Jordanians, and Lebanese started vacationing in the Catskills. Furthermore, the word *Shylock* became a compliment for someone who was manly, an allusion to the famous line: "Am I not a man?" Thus, it was often said of Hollywood hunks: "What a Shylock!" So it happily came to pass that everyone liked Jews. Everyone also liked Muslims. The domino effect, with people liking each other, took over. Things were really good. The only people who still got under everyone's skin were the English, because of their nutty devotion to a powerless, dysfunctional Royal Family, but it was just a minor irritation and nobody went to war about it; they just told the English to get over it and engaged in some hurtful teasing, which wasn't nice, but no death camps were built or anything like that.

THE MOST PHALLIC BUILDING
IN THE WORLD CONTEST

After my diary entry "The Most Phallic Building in the World!" appeared in *Slate,* I began to receive e-mails from readers around the country informing me that my statement about the Williamsburgh Bank Building was incorrect, that there was a building even more phallic in existence and that I had been presumptuous in my claim. They would then proceed to tell me the name of the building which they thought was the most phallic in the world, and this being the Internet age, they would also provide me with a link to a picture of the building.

Well, I received so many e-mails that I decided to have a contest. I sent out a mass e-mail to my mailing list, calling for people to submit links to buildings that they deemed "the most phallic in the world." Somehow the *New York Post* got wind of this and announced my contest on "Page Six," their notorious gossip section. After that, hundreds of e-mails came

my way and the contest grew quite large, so to speak. And it
was a hard decision, so to speak, but I erected, I mean elected,
a real comer, so to speak, which bested my beloved Williamsburgh Bank.

I also invented several categories for the contest, so that
other buildings could be celebrated, and not just the winner.
The other categories were: *Best Uncircumcised Building in the
World; Most Votes; Wrong Contest* (a very Georgia O'Keeffe
building was submitted, if you know what I mean); and *People
Having Relations With Buildings* (some people sent in pictures
that due to camera angles made it appear as if one were looking at a still photo from an architectural version of *Deep
Throat*). After the contest was over, people continued to send
me photos of buildings that they deemed to be the most phallic
in the world, and so I added a final category: *New Comers.*

Luckily, I was able to get my good friends at *Cabinet,* a
brilliant art and culture magazine, to host the contest on their
Web site. We've subsequently received thousands of Internet
visitors, and the contest has been written about in newspapers, magazines, Internet blogs, and architectural journals
all over the world. To see the full results of the contest go to
http://www.cabinetmagazine.org/phallic/contest.php.

What I have for you here is a photo of the Williamsburgh
Bank Building, my inspiration for this whole mad project, and
a picture of the winner of the contest—the Ypsilanti, Michigan, water tower, which is aptly called "The Brick Dick" by
the citizens of that fine town.

2003

The inspiration for the Most Phallic Building in the World Contest:
The Williamsburgh Bank Building, Brooklyn, New York.

The winner of the Most Phallic Building in the World Contest:
The Ypsilanti Watertower, Ypsilanti, Michigan.

'TIS THE SEASON FOR HALITOSIS

There are many upsetting things about the Christmas and New Year's season—increased credit card debt, unresolved decades-long family pain, the spiritual vacuum at the core of our culture—but exposure to bad breath is definitely high on the list.

I recently went to eight Christmas parties in seven days and I was assaulted with so much bad breath that I feel I've gone through four years' worth of dental school and I'm ready to hang a shingle.

I think this must be one of the first things dentists have to be trained for *and* screened for—ability to withstand halitosis. There's probably some kind of machine they put young dentists in front of which blows bad-breath fragrances into their faces until they grow immune, kind of like what they did to that fellow in *Clockwork Orange,* but in reverse. And the dentists who can't take the machine are weeded out and urged to find another field, but certainly not proctology.

In fact, the only people who have it worse than dentists are the proctologists. They're kind of spiritual brothers. The dentist is stationed at the mouth and the proctologist is keeping watch over the ass. I can see them talking to one another through the human body, like children communicating through two cans and a string. The dentist shouts into the mouth, "Hello, down there!"

I once went to a proctologist and desperately wanted to ask him how he could do what he did, but it was one of those questions that you simply can't put out there, though I imagine he would have said something bland like, "It's just another part of the human body."

But can you imagine looking at people's anuses all day long? And mostly at sick anuses? A healthy anus is not appealing—well, to some people it is—but unhealthy ones, the kinds that proctologists have to see, must be very disturbing, even to the most hardened proctologist.

Proctologists for some reason aren't the butt of too many jokes—because we feel bad for them?—but we always make fun of dentists. Yet have we ever put ourselves in *their* green smocks and crepe shoes? Just think of what *they* go through on a daily basis! Garlic breath! Onion breath! Rotting-gum breath! Dull-person breath!

I understand that dentists have a very high rate of suicide, and so I wonder what it's like to be a dentist in Sweden; you'd be doubly burdened. In fact, they probably have a shortage of dentists in that suicide-ravaged country. A mentally strong American dentist could go over there and really earn some cash.

I certainly couldn't be a dentist in America or Sweden. I was so sickened by this one fellow's pâté-breath at one of the Christmas parties I went to that I had to leave early. Later that night—around 3 A.M.—I bolted upright in my bed at the memory of it and couldn't fall back to sleep. I replayed the whole thing, like a barroom fight—a barroom fight that I had lost. The fellow had insisted on crowding me—we were in the kitchen of our mutual friend's home and he had me up against the sink, which was pressing on my sciatic nerve, further paralyzing me.

I should mention that this pâté-fiend had suffered some kind of injury to his larynx as a child and this forces him to whisper all the time, and at this party, which was very loud with the shriekings of overweight children and the gargling noises of alcoholics tipping beers down their throats, he had to get right on top of me to be heard. He was like a boxer getting another boxer against the ropes, but instead of jabs and uppercuts he was scorching my face with such a fierce aroma of partially digested pâté and still-being-chewed pâté that I was sorely tempted to behave in an antisocial manner and say:

"Listen, you're completely unaware of this, lost in the cloud cover of your own id, but you're giving me a second-degree burn with this pâté-breath of yours and I used to sort of like you, but I now feel such repulsion and dislike toward your person that I will snub you for the rest of eternity."

But I didn't say any such thing. I just took a beating and applied the St. Francis prayer: *Better to understand than to be understood, better to forgive than be forgiven.*

What made the moment a little postmodern, despite my use of an old prayer, was that not only was the fellow in question vaporizing me with pâté, he was speaking to me *about* pâté, making my living hell a sort of double hell, like two-dimensional chess.

"What *is* pâté?" he had asked as he shoved a loaded cracker like a cannonball into his mouth.

"Liver," I squeaked.

"Really? I don't like liver, but this stuff is great," he said, firing the cannonball.

"Yes, it's very popular," I aspirated.

"Is it chicken liver?"

"Most likely, though sometimes it's duck liver," I gasped.

Then I thought of a pretty duck floating around in some toxic pond and how the liver filters poison and that I was now breathing in pureed crushed poison that some pretty duck had once absorbed before being slaughtered.

"Excuse me," I then said to him, the vision of this duck floating through my mind, "but I have to go. . . ."

That, I have to say, was probably the zenith of the bad breath I encountered during my holiday party sojourn. After that it was mostly just a lot of bad wine-breath with an occasional kind of universal sour-cheese smell emanating from certain people.

Naturally, I was worried about my own breath at all these parties and was trying to chew a lot of mints, and I was rigorously avoiding hors d'oeuvres, which often come loaded with breath-sabotaging ingredients.

But at one party, I noticed a fellow, as I spoke to him, pull his neck back, spinal notch after spinal notch, like a heron. I was going on about the Bush administration's attempt to quell any kind of protest and I was mostly citing John

Ashcroft's ludicrous case against Greenpeace, but I could hardly make my point as I was secretly thinking that I was dousing the fellow with halitosis and that he was secretly judging me to be a disgusting person.

Oh, we're all so alone!

At another party a rather slobbish fellow spit food directly into my mouth! For some reason my own mouth was open—just for a second, I guess; it was a freak accident—and a particle of food shot right out of him and onto my tongue! It was so disgusting. We both pretended it hadn't happened, but I was deeply mortified and had to swallow the thing like the bitterest of pills.

A few years ago, some kind of white spittle shot out of a person's mouth and attached itself to my cheek and slid down, and we both pretended this had not happened, but having food shot into my mouth was even worse than that white-spittle exchange. When I got home I took three vitamin Cs instead of the recommended dosage of one, and I gargled excessively with Listerine.

At another party the ceilings were very high and no one spit into my mouth *and* I didn't encounter *any* bad breath. As this miracle was unfolding, I wondered if the high ceilings had something to do with it, or was bad breath random, like all other components of the universe? I mean what are the chances of having fifteen meaningless conversations at a Christmas party and not encountering one case of halitosis? But then again, this makes perfect beautiful sense—after all, miracles are what this season is all about.

2003

Science Nonfiction (si'ens non-fik'shen), n. A kind of writing. It was discovered in 2011 that a typographical error at a newspaper over one hundred years earlier had created a profound and great misunderstanding. Brilliant writers, like Jules Verne, Mary Shelley, H. G. Wells, Isaac Asimov, Ray Bradbury, and Philip K. Dick, to name a few, had all along been writing *science NONfiction*. That is, what they were reporting was fact and truth, but a London newspaper review of Verne's work categorized it mistakenly as *science fiction*, leaving out the *non*, and there's been mass confusion ever since. Turns out that time travel, alternative universes, Utopias, helpful robots, space travel, underwater cities, and photon shields had all been accessible to man for quite some time. Cures for every disease and peaceful universes were found to actually exist; there are also gigantic space-eels, who are very disruptive, but they have some very good lasers for those fellows, and they tend to keep to themselves for the most part anyway. Of course, numerous injustices were discovered: A man held in Bellevue at the end of the nineteenth century, purporting to be Captain Nemo, was actually Captain Nemo. His remains, which were found in a potter's field in Queens, New York, have since been transferred to a shrine at the Aquarium in Monterey, California. The good news on that sad story is that at one point during his adventures one of Captain Nemo's mustache hairs was beamed to an alternative universe where people live forever, and from that mustache hair they were able to clone a whole country of Captain Nemos, though some of his new ancestors go by "Lieutenant Nemo." It was also discovered that all episodes of *Star Trek* were actually documentary footage of a real ship, the *Enterprise*. The actor William Shatner, who had claimed all along that he really was Captain Kirk, was glad that the truth had finally come out. (It should be noted that with the revelation that *science fiction* was actually *science nonfiction*, the Vulcan Death-Pinch became a punishable offense, but Vulcans are so essentially kind that they hardly ever use the pinch, except on each other, and on a fellow Vulcan a Vulcan Death-Pinch is only a Vulcan Hurtful-Pinch, and since no other species is able to practice the Death-Pinch, no one has yet been sent to jail for using it, or even been given a ticket.)

KURT COBAIN

When it comes to music I've always been more or less retarded. The first album I ever owned was by Helen Reddy. I don't remember the title. I was ten years old. I heard one of her songs on the radio and I cried. I've always been drawn to things that make me cry—music, movies—even at the age of ten. So I asked my mother to get the record for me and she did. My sister, three and a half years my elder, then immediately and cruelly mocked me for my Reddy fixation, so after one tearful listen I never played the record again.

After that experience, I took the safe route and only listened to what my sister listened to: Joni Mitchell, Cat Stevens, Harry Chapin, Billy Joel, James Taylor, Carol King, and Carly Simon. Why this was so much better than Helen Reddy, I'm not sure.

By the time I was eighteen in 1982, after so much exposure to folk singing, I had no capacity for discerning what was cool music. I was absolutely hopeless, destined to never be able to keep up with my peers when it came to discussing rock bands in a competitive, all-knowing way, which is how white males like to talk about rock 'n' roll. I could argue about baseball players and batting averages with the best of them, but when it came to Led Zeppelin or The Who, I knew nothing.

But I did get into one band during my early-eighties high school life: The Doors. I was a "roadie"—because of having a car with a large trunk—for a band composed of my friends, and all they played were Doors covers at high school parties. When they would sing "Got myself a beer," I would chug as much beer as possible, and then drive the band home drunk later that night. It all felt very romantic at the time.

This Doors period ended, though, with high school, so from 1982 to 1993 I mostly listened over and over to all the folk singers listed above, with occasional intruders, mostly female singers like Suzanne Vega or Natalie Merchant or the Indigo Girls.

You know, it's very embarrassing to be revealing this about myself. It's like saying I'm heterosexual but I'm sitting on a butt plug as I write this.

Then, in 1993, I became aware of this band called Nirvana. Everyone had been making a big deal about them for about a year and I caved into cultural pressure and bought a tape of *Nevermind*. At first it just sounded very loud to me: I was accustomed to the storytelling I heard in folk music or the sweet, sad songs of female vocalists, feeling always that I was in love with the women singers. But then after a few listens to the Nirvana album, it stopped sounding loud to me, and I began to get a taste for something nihilistic and crazed in the music.

I played the tape repeatedly in my car—I didn't have a stereo in the tiny room where I lived, but I had a beat-up Chevy Caprice Classic with a tape deck. My room was pretty far uptown, on the border of Spanish Harlem, and I would drive very fast late at night along the avenues or on the FDR Drive, and the music made me want to be alive in a suicidal way, and I say that without making reference to how Cobain eventually went out. It's genuinely how the songs made me feel: that I had nothing to lose. So, kind of like the way The Doors gave me license—in my mind—to drink too much ten years before, Nirvana now gave me license to do drugs and drive my car really fast and to pursue this crazy girl, whom, fittingly enough, I was crazy about.

Then, after a few months of this attempt at grunge nihilism, I broke up with the girl because I paranoically thought I might have AIDS (I didn't), and by 1994 I was falling apart badly—I had to get sober—and I moved in with my parents in New Jersey. You can only pretend for so long that you have nothing to lose. A lot of times I've acted like I wanted to die, but the will to live has always proved to be much stronger.

Then Cobain killed himself, supposedly because of stomach ulcers. That's what I remember from the news accounts: stomach ulcers and heroin. He was a beautiful boy with his blond hair and sweet face, and now he was dead. I was thirty years old, just a little older than Cobain, and I was safe at home with my mother and father. Down in my parents' basement I watched the TV and I remember the constant video footage of Cobain's misty house. The cameras were always aimed at the windows—or was it glass doors?—next to which his body had been found. How could he have put that gun in his mouth? I wanted to listen to my tape of *Nevermind* to search for clues as to why he really killed himself, but I had lost the album.

Now it's 2004. My son is about to turn eighteen. He hasn't quite inherited my bad taste in music. He's on top of what's happening—he likes all the rap guys. My only influence on him musically is that I did turn him on to The Doors when we took a road trip a year ago. Say what you will about that band, but it is good driving music.

After that trip, we watched the Oliver Stone Doors movie and my son started getting really interested in Jim Morrison, and then he had to do a report on *Apocalypse Now* for his English class and got even more into The Doors, since Coppola uses their music at the end of the film. So we talked a lot about Jim Morrison and I told him that there was this other guy, Kurt Cobain, who was kind of like Morrison, destined to be famous forever because of dying so young.

Then a few weeks ago, my son got *Nevermind* at some garage sale. Leading him to one guy who overdosed on drugs and another guy who committed suicide is really stupid, but my son seems to have a wise, sad take on it—that it's a terrible shame and waste, that it would have been "so cool" if Jim Morrison and Kurt Cobain had made more records.

So this past week we were together for his spring break. We were in his hometown down South, driving around in his pickup truck. We listened a lot to Cobain, and when we didn't have the CD in, the radio stations were playing Nirvana constantly because of the coming anniversary of his death. I liked hearing all the songs again and remembered how Cobain had been my companion in '93, how he made me feel less alone with going crazy. Now I was listening to him with my full-grown son, and my son said more than once, "Yeah, Cobain is cool."

As we kept playing *Nevermind,* I wanted to feel some of the old manic nihilism, but it wasn't there; I couldn't get it back. I was a father sitting next to his son, gently urging him to use his directional signal when he made a turn, or trying, as we talked, to give him decent counsel about his first girl-friend. So I listened to Nirvana and it didn't quite touch me. It didn't make me cry. It didn't make me want to die. It didn't make me do anything except look back. But I was glad to be with my son, listening to music I once loved.

2004

LOOSE TILES

In the late 1960s, when I was a little boy, I used to go to Boro Park, Brooklyn, to visit my grandparents. I was six when they moved from there, so I don't remember too much of the neighborhood or their apartment, and to make things worse my real memories are tangled with memories of photos which I haven't seen for some time.

But there are two things that I recall which don't come from pictures: To get to their apartment, which was on the third floor of a brownstone, I had to climb a long, dark, narrow staircase and about halfway to the top my grandmother, a redhead who usually wore an apron, would come out of her door and appear on the landing, smiling at me, ready to hug me, ready to love me. The second genuine memory is of a small loose tile in the bathroom. The tile was a white rectangle, about two inches long and an inch wide, and it was right next to the toilet and I could nudge and displace it with the toe of my shoe, and then put it back with the toe of my shoe. I liked to do this every time I visited. I liked to see the gap beneath the tile; it was dug out, kind of like a small grave.

What was most remarkable about this piece of tile, which was rather thick and probably ancient, was that in our bathroom back home in New Jersey there was also a loose tile right next to the toilet. No one else in my family (mother, father, older sister) seemed to be aware of this coincidence, and I thought, with the logic of a child, that it must be some shared trait between my mother and her parents, that the two houses were meant to have loose tiles for me to play with. I do remember being very sad when my father changed the tiling in our bathroom and I asked for the loose tile to be returned and my father thought I was joking, or he ignored me; it was some combination of those two responses.

My grandmother was a very good cook and very neat and very unhappy. She collected little antique things made of glass and china. I think they gave her some pleasure. In the mid-1980s, she was diagnosed as having Alzheimer's. She ended up in a nursing home for about a dozen years, sitting in a wheelchair, not thinking, as far as I can tell, and definitely not speaking, though the first year or two she did say one word, over and over, "What? What? What? What?"

She was fed by attendants, a spoon pushed against her lips until she opened her mouth, and she was lifted in and out of bed once or twice a day and put in her wheelchair. I don't know how often they'd bathe her.

On her floor of the nursing home there were many other living-dead sitting in wheelchairs. There seemed to be no care or thought as to how they were placed—behind a door, facing a wall. My grandmother, luckily, was always placed near a window, though she never looked out.

I'd look at the people in the chairs, about forty or fifty of them, and I'd imagine how they were young once—had jobs, love affairs, concerns. I thought they would be disgusted to know what had become of them. And I wondered every time I visited—and I still wonder—if I will be one of those people in a chair someday.

My mother visited my grandmother every month, sometimes less often—the nursing home was in Pennsylvania. I would go once or twice a year and I would watch my mother brush my grandmother's hair, which, with only a few streaks of orange-white, somehow stayed red up until she finally died in 1999 at the age of eighty-nine.

My grandfather was a little heavy and bald and had blue eyes. He was a very sweet, quiet man, but I guess at one time he had a terrible temper. He was about five-nine, not very tall, but there was the implication of a former great strength—he supposedly had carried a small piano on his back into our home in New Jersey, and for many years he was the foreman of a shipping yard, which he ruled with a baseball bat kept under his desk. By the time I knew him, when he was in his late fifties and early sixties, his head had a permanent wobble to it and he was supposedly a reformed drinker. He had shown up once at our house in New Jersey late at night, quite drunk—I was just a baby; this was around 1965—and my mother told him he had to quit drinking or he would never see me or my sister again. After that night, no one ever did see him take another drink. But when he died of a rotted gut in 1981, at the age of seventy-two, we found many vodka bottles hidden beneath his worktable.

In 1971, my grandparents, whom I called Nanny and Poppy, moved from Brooklyn to Williamsport, Pennsylvania, because my uncle, my mother's brother, lived there, and because Brooklyn was changing. They got a cute little house on a corner, and I guess there was the hope that they would be happy.

My grandmother had wanted a house for years, longing for her childhood in Saratoga Springs, New York, and the big house she had grown up in. That house in Saratoga was on Lincoln Street, and this new house in Pennsylvania was also on Lincoln Street. This was supposed to be a good sign. But I guess it wasn't. It must have been too late to go back to her childhood, or there was no going back, anyway. Or maybe she did. If she had recalled correctly, she would have realized her childhood had been tragic and difficult—her mother died when she was eleven and she had to drop out of school and raise her brothers, with the help of her sister, my great-aunt Doris. So my grandmother was consistent—a miserable childhood, a miserable old age.

In 1972, my grandfather left her in the car with the engine running, while he was doing a quick errand, but something went wrong—the car wasn't in park, perhaps; this mystery was never solved—and she and the car slid through the plate-glass window of a store. Her back was wrenched, she was in pain for years—maybe until the Alzheimer's robbed her of all sensation—and she never forgave my grandfather for this.

She had never forgiven him for anything, though, so this was nothing new, but I guess this car accident was the final blow. Whereas once they had fought, now they hardly spoke to one another; she gave him a sort of silent treatment up until he died in 1981.

So in that new house, they slept in separate bedrooms, and she made him build a shower and toilet in the basement; she didn't want her beautiful new bathroom soiled (she had hated, it turns out, the old rotting tiles in Brooklyn). She could use the upstairs bathroom and shower—she must have scrubbed it down immediately afterward—but he was not allowed. The Alzheimer's may have kicked in earlier than we realized—I've read that one of the first symptoms of Alzheimer's is an obsession with cleanliness, and she had always had that, but it got worse and worse.

My grandfather, who, like my grandmother, never went to high school, was secretly smart, I think. He'd write my mother and me and my sister two-page letters in beautiful cursive writing, always ending with the phrase "And on we go." To bring in some money in his retirement, he worked flea markets, selling old coins and pocket watches that he had repaired at his workbench. He would write in his letters, tragicomically, "I'm nothing but a peddler."

Sometimes I'd stay with them in Williamsport. My grandfather bought me a bicycle. It was orange with a black seat. It was a pretty good bike, not great. The front tire would rub in a funny way and that was never fixed, but I liked riding it on the uneven sidewalks of Lincoln Street.

Now, when I visit my uncle in Williamsport, I walk past my grandparents' little house, empty of them for a long time now, but I'd like to go in there and find them and talk to them. I always want the dead to come back to life, but they never do. I have often thought of going to Boro Park and finding the old brownstone—maybe I could conjure them up there—but I never go. The result would be the same: no ghosts, no living people, no one to love whom I had once loved.

I can see it, though: a sidewalk, a brownstone, a concrete front staircase, and a closed front door. And behind the door, a narrow staircase that probably wouldn't seem very steep to me now as I climbed it, and there would be no one coming onto the landing to greet me, unless it was to ask what I was doing in their home.

2004

SNEAKERS MAKE THE BOY

As a young boy I had a shoe fetish. Not to brag, but I was clearly something of a prodigy when it comes to perversion, and my shoe fetish, like most perversions, had a ritualistic aspect, because the whole thing with perversion is buildup, creating a mounting order for the revelation of forbidden delights. Think of the man (a panty fetishist) who steals panties from female acquaintances:

Step 1: He seizes an opportunity—at a dinner party, let's say—to gain access into the acquaintance's bedroom. Then he opens bureau drawers and his heart is pounding deliciously with adrenaline.

Step 2: He finds the panty drawer—bliss. He hesitates—the glory of the moment: all those panties!—and then his hand shoots into the drawer.

Step 3: He grabs a pair of panties, hides them on his person. He then sneaks out of the bedroom and is narcotized for the rest of the evening, somehow making polite conversation.

Steps 4 and 5: When he gets home, he delays gratification—he clears dishes from the sink, makes phone calls, washes up. Then he gets into bed and examines the panties thoroughly and puts them on or just stares at them, and in either case manipulates himself to orgasm. Of course, what follows is terrible despair and acid self-loathing and promises to himself that this is the last time!

Well, my shoe thing as a boy wasn't as bad as the fetish described above, but for me getting a new pair of sneakers—my shoe fetish was, to be precise, more of a sneaker fetish—was so stimulating, so exciting, that I could barely contain myself. I wasn't capable of orgasm, at least the mature male orgasm that I know of today, but I would have the equivalent of a female orgasm—where the body vibrates for some time like a tuning fork that's been struck. I would bring the new sneakers home and lock myself in my room, and for hours my hands would examine, like a crazed connoisseur, the unmarked soles—and all the while I'd be tingling madly.

Over the months to come, I would continue to erotically examine and touch the soles, watching them as they degraded over time, their little crevices and swishes and jagged edges reduced to smooth flat rubber which was very pleasing to caress.

When I would first get a new pair of sneakers, I would also passionately sniff at them, intoxicating myself with the perfume of the new rubber. Another thing I did was respectfully keep my sneakers, for the first week or so, in their box—they were too new and precious to just be casually left on the floor when I took them off. And when I went to sleep at night, I would put the box by my bed, with the top off, like a coffin at a Catholic wake. I left the box open so that even as I slept I could breathe in the sneakers' fragrance, which only lasted a few days. Also, I liked to stare at my sneakers right up until the point I passed out—my night-light providing just enough illumination.

Why was I so into sneakers? Well, there was, obviously, the tactile part: I loved the rubber, the *feel* of the rubber. Why this is I don't know, but I may have been learning how to use my sense of touch, the way we learn what we like to eat by tasting different foods. There was also, as I described above, that incredible new-sneaker smell. And I must have loved that bouquet, because I associated it with the tremendous feeling of hope that came with new sneakers—that with this pair I would run faster, have greater adventures, more fun.

And, finally, as a last attempt to understand my sneaker love affair, I know that like children today I took my identity from my sneakers, whether, depending on the year, they were Keds or Pumas or Converse or Adidas (I'm of the pre-Nike generation). So, you see, with my "cool" sneakers, I could face the world. They were both my shield and, if I needed to flee, my means of escape. It is the childhood version of the way adults judge themselves and others by the cars they drive.

But other people didn't perceive my sneakers the way I did. I vividly remember this time in the sixth grade when I was playing basketball—one-on-one—with the best player in my class. He was a tall, brutish fellow and he was surprised at how well I played—I was a straight-A student—and he jockishly complimented me: "I didn't think you would be good."

But I was surprised by his surprise. I thought he should have noted before we began playing that I was wearing my special Adidas basketball sneakers with their red, white, and blue stripes, and that this should have indicated to him, despite my straight-A reputation, that only a good player would have such sneakers. I even said to him, in response to his backhanded compliment: "But didn't you see my sneakers?"

"What are you talking about?"

"I'm wearing Adidas," I said.

"So what," he said. Then we finished playing and he won, and I have to say that after that I never quite got the same thrill from a new pair of sneakers. It wasn't because I lost the game—he was the best player in my class and much taller than me and I had expected to lose—but because I had learned that my sneakers didn't change what anybody thought about me. Up until that moment, I hadn't known that, and, in fact, had thought the opposite. I thought my sneakers told everybody who I was.

Recently, over twenty-five years later, I crossed paths with the guy I had played basketball with. He still lives in my hometown and we met at a meeting for people with drinking problems. He's still big, and he doesn't have a gut, but he's very filled out and he still has his hair. He does construction. He's a humble ex-jock, working on his drinking problem. I'm bald and a writer, and I'm working on my drinking problem. We've both ended up in the same place. Who would have thought it? The straight-A student and the basketball star. He was happy to see me. We shook hands. He remembered my name. I wanted to ask him if he remembered our one-on-one game, but I was sure he didn't, so I held my tongue. But seeing him again made me think of those Adidas sneakers. I feel like running out and getting a pair. I've heard they've come back into style.

2004

Talkies (tok'eez), n. A cinematic projection of a story involving human beings who talk to one another and don't try to kill each other. This was a word that had briefly flourished in the late 1920s with the advent of sound in cinema, but was eventually dropped from the OED as the age of "silent pictures" (the converse of *talkies*) was more or less forgotten. Then, in 2022, movies started to be officially called "killies," since all films were now about killing. Then, in 2033, rebel filmmakers began to make small, underground, humanistic dramas in which people actually talked and no firearms or piercing weapons were allowed; it was a strict form of cinema and the word *talkies* came back into being, though with a slightly different connotation than its earlier meaning, which simply referred to "talking" that could be *heard*, whereas *talkies* now implied a whole worldview (pacifistic in nature). By 2054, these underground films had become so popular that they replaced "killies" as the leading form of cinematic entertainment.

A TRIBUTE TO
GEORGE PLIMPTON AND
HIS NOVEL *THE CURIOUS CASE*
OF SIDD FINCH[10]

When I have insomnia, I play out in my mind wonderful fantasies. But I should qualify something—they are not erotic, these reveries, they are heroic, though that's not to say that erotic fantasies can't be heroic for those of you who go in for that sort of thing.

My insomnia fantasies fall into three categories:
(1) Baseball prowess/heroics.
(2) Basketball prowess/heroics.
(3) General heroism.
    (a) Saving a woman.

[10] George Plimpton, the longtime editor of the *Paris Review* and the author of numerous books, died on September 26, 2003.

(b) Saving a small child or several small children from a burning building.

The baseball fantasy goes like this: One day I wake up with great strength and wildly heightened reflexes, but I don't know this. I'm sort of like Franz Kafka's Gregor Samsa, but much more positive. The day I awaken with my superpowers, I happen to go to the batting cage at Coney Island for some amusement. I step into the 50-mph cage, my usual speed, and I crush every ball. Sensing that something is up, I venture into the 75-mph cage and again crush every ball. I then go into the 90-mph cage and it's like the machine is pitching softballs. I hit a batting-cage home run every time.

The fantasy then fast-forwards to my getting a tryout with the Yankees, even though I'm thirty-nine years old, weigh 150 pounds—all of which is meagerly distributed on a six-foot frame—and last played organized baseball in the ninth grade. From the tryout, which leaves the Yankees scouts and coaching staff absolutely astounded, I make the team as a pinch hitter, and eventually—well, rather quickly—earn a regular spot in the lineup. I then mentally compile my statistics for the season, though it's hard to not allow myself to hit 1.000. But I want to keep things fairly realistic, so I merely hit .412 with 58 home runs and 195 RBIs, thinking that such numbers are beautiful, it being the nature of a baseball fan to find numbers and statistics beautiful. If you'll notice, I only break the all-time single-season RBI record, previously held by Hack Wilson, because I humbly don't want to make a mockery of the game and be that much superior to my peers, though of course I am the first person to hit .400 since Ted Williams.

I do have to admit I somewhat prefer my basketball fantasy to my baseball fantasy, because I delusionally feel that it is within the realm of the possible. I never was a very good baseball player—my career Little League average is less than half my fantasy average: about .190, I'd guess—but I am a fairly good basketball player, if I may say so. I'm in possession of a better-than-average jump shot, and this makes the basketball fantasy nearly believable, at least at four o'clock in the morning when I can't sleep.

The way the fantasy works is this: I begin to take yoga classes, and in doing so some kind of life-energy is released from my perpetually stiff lower back and absolutely inflexible hamstrings, which are more like ham-ropes. So the yoga transforms me and I go out to my local playground court and find that I can dunk. I then get a tryout with the New York Knicks and they're amazed to see an unknown middle-aged novelist jump like a young Michael Jordan. I make the team and we win the championship, with me dunking the winning basket over two, maybe three defenders. An added bonus to the basketball fantasy is that my shiny head, which I shave because of my balding, fits in perfectly with the preferred hairstyle of my fellow NBAers, and so my hair loss is no longer a source of shame for me.

Compared with my exploits in the sports world, my general heroic fantasies are pretty standard stuff. I walk past a burning house, dash into it, and carry out many children, maybe a whole orphanage. Then I'm hospitalized with smoke inhalation and the next day a picture of me in my hospital bed is on the front page of the *New York Post* with the headline: *HERO!*

Or I'm walking home one day and I hear a scream. I dash into an apartment building vestibule and discover a man terrorizing a woman. But before the man is able to do anything, I have arrived on the scene and engage in an epic battle with the marauder, who is absolutely enormous and fearsome. During our fight, he stabs me, but I'm able to knock him out and then tie him up until the police arrive. The woman, who looks like Grace Kelly at the zenith of her beauty, is incredibly grateful and holds me in her arms while I bleed profusely from my wound. I lose a lot of blood and I'm rushed to the hospital, where I nearly die, but I pull through. The mayor of New York visits me in the hospital and the headline in the *Post* reads: *WRITER SAVES WOMAN!* I then sometimes indulge myself with the idea that my book sales will greatly increase after my heroic deed and the subsequent press coverage; I also like to think that maybe I get a tough-guy scar on my cheek from the fight.

Well, enough with my fantasies. I've only laid this out for you to show you that I have specific psychological insight as to how and why George Plimpton created the marvelous character Sidd Finch, who is possibly the greatest pitcher of all time, real or imagined. You see, George *wanted* to be Sidd Finch, in the same way that all these years, I've wanted to break Hack Wilson's RBI record. He *dreamed* of being Sidd Finch. He says as much in his first baseball book (and his first book) *Out of My League:*

. . . *I began to be plagued by those half-forgotten boyhood dreams of heroics on the major league baseball diamonds, so many of them flooding my mind.* . . .

So, plagued by these stirred-up dreams, George Plimpton, in 1960, went to his editor at *Sports Illustrated* and pitched the idea (so to speak) that he should take the mound against major leaguers in an all-star game and then write about it. Here's the dialogue of George's pitch to his editor, Sid James, as George reported it in *Out of My League:*

"I pitched at school," I told him, "and at college a bit, and once or twice in the army. But the point is," I went on, "that I would pitch not as a hotshot—that'd be a different story—but as a guy who's average, really, a sort of Mr. Everybody, the sort who thinks he's a fair athlete, a good tennis player, but always finds himself put out in the second round of the club tournament by the sandy-haired member who wears a hearing-aid."

"I see," he said.

There was a leather sofa behind me and I sat down in it. "James Thurber," I said obliquely, "once wrote that the majority of American males put themselves to sleep by striking out the batting order of the New York Yankees. That's my fellow, you see, lying there staring at the bedroom ceiling . . . the bases loaded, and he's imagining himself coming in from the bullpen. . . ."

Don't let George's displacement about the "American male" and "that's my fellow" throw you off; he's also the American male who stared at his ceiling, fantasizing. George Plimpton was a college pitcher who continued to dream, long after college was over, of pitching greatness. And so was born, I contend, the character of Sidd Finch—born on the screen of a bedroom ceiling, long before the character actually came to the page.

And when Sidd did come to the page, what an incredible debut it was. On April 1, 1985, George wrote an article for *Sports Illustrated* about a rookie pitcher for the Mets, one Sidd ("two D's for Siddhartha") Finch, who was a Buddhist monk-in-training and could throw a fastball at 168 mph. Sidd pitched with one bare foot and one foot in a work boot, had spent years in Tibet, and played the French horn.

Well, this April Fools' Day hoax worked better than anyone expected. Sports pages all over the country reported that the Mets had the greatest phenom ever. Eventually, the truth came out, and a number of readers of *Sports Illustrated* canceled their subscriptions, feeling they had been duped and mistreated, though most, of course, got a kick out of the looniness of it all. Then, two years later, George published the only novel he ever wrote, *The Curious Case of Sidd Finch*, providing the world with the full story of the amazing young pitcher.

One of my brilliant theories is that George made Finch a Buddhist monk-in-training—it's his Buddhist practices that give Finch his great pitching abilities—because George must have imagined that he himself could somehow be a great pitcher if he just meditated correctly. It's like my yoga fantasy. I think we come up with such notions because we realize that our bodies will never be able to do the things we'd like, but if somehow we could bypass the body through the spirit, then the Jonathan Ameses of the world could dunk, and the George Plimptons/Sidd Finches of the world could strike out the Yankees, could strike out the world!

I think, too, that maybe George made Finch a Buddhist because he himself was perhaps a fledgling Buddhist, which may come as a surprise to the people who saw George presiding over *Paris Review* parties in his blue blazer, since one doesn't usually associate blue blazers with Buddhism. But I think this might be the case, since George certainly was living proof of one of the Buddhist mantras he presents in *The Curious Case of Sidd Finch*. It is a mantra which is meant to help with writer's block and goes like this: *Om Ara Ba Isa Na Dhi*. It means: Living ripens verbal intelligence. Sidd Finch prescribes this mantra to Robert Temple, the narrator of *The Curious Case of Sidd Finch*, who, naturally, suffers from writer's block. Well, if there ever was an example that living ripens verbal intelligence, it was George Plimpton. He was so curious, so amused, so alive, so enchanted by the whimsical and the absurd and the fantastic, that all of this came bursting out in his incredible writing, with its inimitable mix of the comedic and the graceful.

To further plunder this Buddhist-spiritual theme, I'd venture to say that George Plimpton was practically enlightened, or, rather, he was literally enlightened—the fellow, this extraordinary Mr. Everybody, seemed to *glow*. If he was present in a room you spotted him immediately and your eye was drawn to him—his silver hair ("silver mop" might be the better description) was a beacon, you couldn't miss it, it was everywhere, like the smile of the Mona Lisa. And should you come face-to-face with the man, there was pouring out of George a generosity of spirit that was so great that it seemed to have a physical quality: light. Jack Kerouac gives a description in *On the Road* of the kind of people he was wild for, and I think it's the perfect depiction of George, especially considering George's great love of fireworks:

. . . the only people for me are the mad ones, the ones who are mad to live, mad to talk, mad to be saved, desirous of everything at the same time, the ones who never yawn or say a commonplace thing, but burn, burn, burn like fabulous yellow roman candles exploding like spiders across the stars and in the middle you see the blue centerlight pop and everybody goes "Awww!"

That was my experience when I met George: I was in awe and I said, "Awww!" Shaking his hand was like shaking the hand of literature in the twentieth century. I met him in the spring of 1999 at a storytelling performance in which we were both involved, and to my surprise he had read some of my essays, though I don't think he was aware that for a few years I had been calling myself "The George Plimpton of the Colon." I had given myself this sobriquet because I had gone for a colonic with the sole purpose of writing about it. But then, in the fall of 1999, a few months after meeting George, I pursued something a bit more Plimptonesque: I had an amateur boxing match. When I started training for the fight, part of my regimen was to read George's *Shadowbox*, which is his memoir about his famous encounter in the ring with the light-heavyweight Archie Moore.

Well, I broke my nose while sparring nine days before my fight but still went through with the thing, and my nose was rebroken in the second round. But to my credit I lasted all four scheduled rounds, though I lost the fight. A few days after the bout, I went to one of George's *Paris Review* parties that he held in his home and I showed off to him my fractured nose and two black eyes. He very much approved, and was happy that an Ames had entered the ring, and was going to report as much to that side of his family. We were not related, but George's mother was an Ames. His middle name was Ames.

George also approved, I think, of the fact that I lost. Winning is good for fantasies and late-night insomnia, but losing is good for writing—it's more interesting, more humorous, more human. And being good at losing was one of George's many gifts. He had the bearing of General MacArthur, but the soul of Charlie Chaplin. He was wildly brave and intrepid, fearless really, but he was also gleefully self-deprecating at the same time. So he liked the fact that I had broken my nose in defeat. Archie Moore, after all, had broken George's nose.

A few weeks after that *Paris Review* party I went to Cuba. In *Shadowbox*, George wrote several memorable passages about being in Havana with Hemingway. He describes going to Hemingway's favorite bar, the Floridita, where Papa (how George referred to him) sat in the corner with a bust of his own likeness behind him and how talking to Papa there was a strange double-fold encounter. He also reported about the time he brought Tennessee Williams to the Floridita to meet Papa, and how the meeting had been awkward—Hemingway didn't know what to make of Williams. So I went to that bar and sat near the corner, which is now roped off to protect that bust of Hemingway, and I imagined George and Hemingway and Williams sitting there. I pretended to be in the past. I liked it in the past.

Then I went to Hemingway's house, where George had written about having drinks with Hemingway on the patio. Papa had thrown a punch at him after challenging George to spar by saying, "Let's see how good you are." So as I looked at Hemingway's patio, I pictured George there. Young and tall and handsome. I saw him, in my mind, taking on the side of his head Papa's left hook. It would have been bad manners not to let the great man hit him.

When I've traveled over the years, I've gone to Venice looking for Thomas Mann, to Spain for Hemingway, to Berlin for Christopher Isherwood, to Denver for Jack Kerouac, to

Big Sur for Henry Miller. And in Cuba I went looking for George Plimpton. But I never told George that, and I regret this. It would have been a way to let him know how much I admired him, how much I worshiped him, how much I adored him. But one rarely says these sorts of things, though I wish I had. I should mention that I never found any of those writers when I went looking for them, and I didn't really find George in Cuba, but I did find him in New York, and for that I will always be grateful.

2004

I LOVE JACK KEROUAC

The question was: What book has most influenced you? And right away, I thought of Kerouac's *On the Road*. It didn't influence my writing, but it influenced my life, and I'm certainly not alone with this. Over the years, Kerouac has turned on hundreds of thousands of young people. In fact, on the cover of my worn Signet paperback copy, beneath the title, are these two sentences: *One of the most powerful and important novels of our time. The book that turned on a generation.*

Now this is just book-cover hyperbole, but I think its truth is somewhat indisputable. Kerouac is a major literary and cultural figure of the twentieth century, despite what the naysayers naysay. I do concede that the phrase "turned on" is a bit antiquated, but it's the best I—and the people at Signet, who are probably dead now—can come up with.

I purchased the book in 1981 when I was seventeen. I went to the Walden Bookstore in the Wayne Hills Mall in

Wayne, New Jersey, and I still have my original copy. The cost in the top right-hand corner of the book is $2.50. There's no picture on the cover, just an image of the sun. It might actually be a photograph of the sun or a really good painting of the sun. The top and middle part of the book, which has Kerouac's name and the title, is sort of a brown color, and then the lower third of the book fades to orange because of the glow of the sun. I feel compelled to describe the book itself since it is right next to me, between my arms as I type, in the space between the keyboard and the end of the desk.

I've had this book for twenty-three years. Other than my Tarzan novels and my Tolkien books, the cherished books of my adolescence, I've not held on to any other book for so long.

Here are the circumstances of my buying *On the Road:*

I was taking fencing lessons at New York University. I was living in New Jersey and would take the bus into the city. This sounds very Holden Caulfieldish, but he was the manager of his fencing team, whereas I was an actual fencer. Like Holden, though, I was a bit disturbed. I was an unhappy seventeen-year-old. Due to whatever middle-class psychic-emotional disturbances that existed in my home, I would lie in bed at night and have one of three fantasies:

(1) Suicide, usually by hanging, since a boy in my hometown hung himself.

(2) Smashing my house with a baseball bat—the windows and the furniture.

(3) Running away from home by hitchhiking to California, where I would work as a busboy in a restaurant, possibly to be discovered by Hollywood. If that happened, I would then become a movie star like my hero Steve McQueen. And

it wasn't so much that I wanted to be a movie star, but to be like the characters Steve McQueen played—tough guys who had some kind of sweet-wounded look in their eyes.

Anyway, after my weekly fencing lesson at NYU, which ended around 8 P.M., I would get drunk in the bars on Bleecker Street in the West Village. The bartenders didn't card me and I would polish off several beers. Then I would get on the subway to the Port Authority, where I'd catch a ten o'clock bus home. My mother had me taking the lessons so that I would excel at fencing and get into an Ivy League school. She didn't know that I was wiping out whatever I had learned in my lessons by getting drunk. Like I said, I was unhappy. I was young. A lot of young people are unhappy. So are older people. So are middle-aged people. I'm middle-aged now, but I'm neither happy nor unhappy. I'm confused and frightened, but not overwhelmingly so. I get by.

So one night in the darkened bus back to New Jersey there was this guy in an army jacket. He had long hair and a beard, and there was a large green duffel bag at his feet. He looked like a hippie. We were both sitting in the last row— he was across from me. I knew that hippies engaged in hitchhiking, which had always intrigued me. Did anyone really get around that way? There weren't too many hippies left by 1981, but there were a few stragglers still hanging on from the 1970s, and when we went on family trips, I would sometimes see these hippies on the side of the highway with their cardboard signs, their destinations written out in thick black letters. So even though this hippie was on a *bus,* I asked him the following question (the beers I had drunk gave me courage):

"Excuse me. Can I ask you something? Do you know how to hitchhike? Is it safe?"

One of my problems with fantasy number three above was that I was uncertain if hitchhiking actually worked—I never saw anyone stop for hippies—and my parents, whenever we passed those hitchhikers, usually said something about how dangerous it was, how there were a lot of sick people on the roads.

The guy said: "Yeah, I know how to hitchhike. It's okay. But if you want to know about it just get this book, *On the Road,* by Jack Kerouac."

It sounded like he said "Carrow-wacky" and I thought he might be bullshitting me—he wasn't very friendly and he told me about the book as a way to get out of talking to me. But the next day I went to the bookstore and sure enough I found *On the Road,* and that night and in the days to come, I had that quintessential young-person reading experience: I wasn't alone. There was someone who felt just like me. Someone who wanted to bust out. Someone who wanted terribly to be free.

The book, for those of you who haven't read it, is an autobiographical novel, capturing Kerouac's years of hitchhiking and driving all around America in the late 1940s. Kerouac is considered the father of the Beat Generation, the coiner of the phrase itself, and he had legendary friendships with many writers, most notably the poet Allen Ginsberg and the novelist William Burroughs. Kerouac's most famous friendship, though, was with Neal Cassady, who wrote only one book, *The First Third.* Cassady was a gigantic figure for the Beats—a wild man of energy and madness. In the sixties, he was the driver of Ken Kesey's Merry Prankster bus, a trip immortalized in Tom Wolfe's book *The Electric Kool-Aid Acid Test*. More important, Cassady is the hero of several of Kerouac's novels, including *On the Road*.

And so I was seventeen, in desperate need of guidance, of something, and on the fifth page of *On the Road*, I read these lines from Kerouac, a description of Cassady and Ginsberg:

They rushed down the street together, digging everything in the early way they had, which later became so much sadder and perceptive and blank. But then they danced down the streets like dingledodies, and I shambled after as I've been doing all my life after people who interest me, because the only people for me are the mad ones, the ones who are mad to live, mad to talk, mad to be saved, desirous of everything at the same time, the ones who never yawn or say a commonplace thing, but burn, burn, burn like fabulous yellow roman candles exploding like spiders across the stars and in the middle you see the blue centerlight pop and everybody goes "Awww!"

And then two pages later, I read these lines:

I was a young writer and I wanted to take off.

Somewhere along the line I knew there'd be girls, visions, everything; somewhere along the line the pearl would be handed to me.

Well, just like the book-cover hyperbole said, I was turned on. I wanted to burn, burn, burn. I wanted to shamble after people. I wanted to be shambled after. I was desirous of everything at once, just like he said. But what to do? How to do it? How to find the pearl? How to find what Kerouac simply called "it"? How to take off?

Well, my method was to try to be like Kerouac himself. I drove somebody's van to Denver after seeing their notice on a wall at a youth hostel in New York. Then I went to the Jack Kerouac School of Disembodied Poetics in Boulder, Colorado, but couldn't afford any of the classes. I hitchhiked in Europe and a little in the U.S., but I could still hear my parents' words of caution, so I was a little scared to hitchhike too much. I was Kerouacish on the outside, but somewhat Woody Allenish on the inside. Mostly, I busted out by drinking more and smoking more pot. When really intoxicated, I would tell strangers that my name was Jack, and sometimes I stayed in flop hotels and when I did I would always sign the ancient registers as Jack Kerouac. I wanted, somehow, to bring him back to life.

Toward the end of my run of trying to be a latter-day Jack K.—this was the summer of 1986—I ran into Allen Ginsberg on the street in New York. He was in his early sixties, bald with a gray professorial beard. He was no longer a young dingledodie. I spotted him just as he was coming out of a bar on Avenue A. It was late at night, and he was with a young man. I bravely went up to him and said, "Can I talk to you about Jack Kerouac?" How rude of me! I didn't even pretend to be interested in his poetry. But he was kind to me, said he would talk to me. I had a million questions, but blurted out something along the lines of: "It seems like Kerouac wrote straight from the heart." And he told me that Kerouac revised his writing a lot more than people knew, and then he asked me where I went to school. "Princeton," I said. And then he reached out and stroked my cheek and he smiled and said, "You look like a Princeton boy."

The young man next to him had a sweet, accepting look on his face. I then offered Allen Ginsberg a beer—I had two six-packs on me; I was on my way to a party—but he graciously didn't take one and then he said he had to go and so we parted. I was a little disappointed, but at least I'd had a few moments with him, and then he turned around and called out to me and wagged his finger at me and said, "Be careful!" This made me think that maybe he saw I was a kindred spirit to Kerouac and Cassady—someone who should be careful, since Kerouac died from alcoholism at age forty-seven and Cassady from drugs at age forty-four.

So at first Ginsberg's admonition made me feel proud. I was like Kerouac and Cassady! But then it began to haunt me. My drinking, even at twenty-two, was getting worse, and I wondered if I was doomed and if Ginsberg had seen this. I had recently reread *On the Road* and had begun to form a different take on the book. During my first read, at seventeen, mostly what I caught was the exuberance of it all—Kerouac describing his soul as "whoopeing." But after my second read in 1986, I saw that he was writing about something that had already passed; in fact, in the lines above, he hinted at it, but I hadn't seen it—"which later became so much sadder and perceptive and blank."

I came to think that Kerouac's prescription in *On the Road* for finding "it," or rather, my prescription of trying to be like him to find "it," was a suicide path. That I'd end up just like Kerouac, who died while living with his mother, choking to death on his own blood from an alcoholic hemorrhage in his throat.

Sure enough, a year later, in 1987, I was on a locked ward in a hospital for a week, and then I was transferred to the substance abuse unit. There I told the group my "life story," how I had for years wanted to be like Jack Kerouac. And my roommate, a toll clerk on the Garden State Parkway who had lost his job because of cocaine and was a mean, twisted little man, derisively called me Jack for the rest of my stay. He didn't know that Jack Kerouac was a real writer—he thought I had multiple personality disorder, "like Sybil." So somebody was calling me Jack, just as I had always wanted, but now it was for the wrong reasons.

Eventually I got out of that hospital—the doctor told me I was a maniac, but it was an incorrect diagnosis—and I became a writer. I stopped trying to be like Kerouac, but I didn't stop loving him. I'd go to bookstores and look at the biographies of him, just for the black-and-white pictures in the middle. It was like visiting his grave; I was mourning him. I still mourn him. I still love him. He was my friend when I needed one at age seventeen; he inspired me to want to live, to go crazy, to desire everything at once. It was an Icarus path, one of flying too close to the sun, like the sun on the cover of the book. But he did teach me to fly for a while, and even though I burned and crashed and have walked along the ground ever since or have crawled, I still look up at the skies— I still go to bookstores and look at his pictures and I marvel at him and love him, and I will never forget him.

2004

OUR SELVES BETWEEN US

It's my opinion that my heart is rather broken. But that implies that I have a heart. I guess I do, but it's a totally flawed heart. It doesn't work for shit. I don't know how to love. I'm forty years old. I'm bald. I think my penis has stopped working. My fingernails are all ridged and dying. A sun-blemish on my shoulder ripped open the other day and was bleeding. That can't be good. I probably have skin cancer on my shoulder and it's eating its way through me as I type.

I've been crying for the last hour and not because of skin cancer, but because I was listening to the mixed tape that my love made for me. It takes devotion to make a mixed tape, and it's a dying art. Sneaking off with someone's iPod and downloading songs on the sly is not quite the same thing, but I imagine that it's the wave of the future.

So the tape really made me cry. I figured that all the songs were like her singing to me. For part of the tape, I sat at the kitchen table where we used to sit. I sat in her chair. I've almost never sat in that chair and I've lived in this apartment for five years. The floor is at a weird angle by that chair. But for two years she sat there. I also gave her the bad side of the bed. She made those sacrifices. She wanted to be in my bed and she liked for us to eat together. I often felt rushed, though, when we had meals. I didn't want to take the time to sit down and eat properly. But I would. And a lot of times, I would try to correct her posture. She told me I could. She has bad posture and she wanted me to remind her to straighten up. She's beautiful, but when she sits to eat, she slumps terribly, curves her spine. I never should have tried to get her to sit right. It was wrong of me.

So sitting there now, listening to the tape, missing her, I was starting to lose it, and then I heard this lyric—"We sat here with our selves between us." It's from a John Cale song, "Anda Lucia," and when I heard that line I really started weeping. It made me think of the two of us sitting there, trapped, our selves blocking us from being able to love, the way all selves block all love. How do you get past the self?

Then I was back in the moment and the kitchen was empty—it's a mess now that she's gone. The sink dirty, the floor dirty. Everything barren and stained. I'm forty and I can't take care of myself. Or, rather, I'm too lazy to take care of myself.

So she moved out two months ago. It was a hard decision we came to. I moved in with my parents to give her time, and then I paid for her move. Big deal. When I came back to the apartment, the first thing I saw was her empty closet. It had been filled with her pretty clothes for two years. That empty closet was like a grave. A death. An end. I started crying bad. I took one look at it and ran to the bed and cried facedown in the pillow. I'm halfway through life and have no idea how to live.

There's this scene in Richard Yates's book *Revolutionary Road* which is the most painful thing I've ever read. This neglectful husband has lost his wife to suicide. He goes into her closet and smells her clothes and for a moment he has her back, he can smell her, she's there, not dead, and he feels all the love he had for her, the love which had been lost, and then this horrible intrusive neighbor is banging on the door, and the husband hides in the closet until the neighbor leaves, but the spell has been broken, he can't get his wife back, he tries, but he can't reconjure her and he's lost her for good now, and this second death is worse than the first.

So when I got off the bed, done crying, I waved my hand in that empty closet to see if it was real. To see if I had really lost something so precious, and my hand sliced through the air and I knew I had lost her and I went back to the bed and cried some more. Just recently I put some of my raggedy clothes in there and they look ugly. They look like me.

2004

Truespapers (trooz'pa'perz), n. A journal printed on paper, usually once a day, though sometimes there are multiple editions; such a journal usually contains information about current events, provides reviews of various forms of entertainment, has numerous advertisements for brassieres and hair loss, offers commentary in the form of editorials, publishes comics, and makes people's hands dirty, which is a well-known tie-in with the soap industry. In 2009, it was discovered that 83 percent of the content of all *newspapers* was false; the 17 percent of true material was found to exist only in the gossip sections, like the famed "Page Six" of the *New York Post,* and in the sports pages with their reports of scores, though it was later discovered that all the scores were fabricated and the games themselves elaborate ruses, but that the reporting of the scores was honest. It was learned that all sports became false when nobody could take the stress anymore of unknown outcomes—too many coaches were having heart attacks and numerous players were developing colitis. So the suffering coaches and players got together and fixed the outcomes. As of the printing of this dictionary, the sports world continues to be false, but people still enjoy watching. Anyway, once it was learned that newspapers were full of untruths, a graphic juicer, called the *Honestizer,* was invented; all newspapers were then channeled through this elaborate juicer and true reports were synthesized. To reassure the public that they were now getting the truth, newspapers had their names officially changed to *truespapers* in 2010. Unfortunately, people found the new journals exceedingly boring and sales went way down; but the upshot was that a lot of trees got to live and there was a notable decrease in global warming. So all in all it was a positive development. The truth was out and the temperatures were down.

HOW I ALMOST COMMITTED SUICIDE BECAUSE OF A WART

In 1984, when I was twenty years old, I had a wart on my penis. This is not uncommon. Most Americans have warts on their genitals, according to the medical journals, but the sheer plurality and popularity of the wart doesn't make it an attractive condition. But there *is* a certain solace in the numbers, in not being alone with this affliction.

Anyway, in 1984 a dermatologist in my hometown burned off the wart, employing something that looked like a high-tech cigarette lighter. Before burning me, though, he sunk a needle into my penis that was larger than my penis. My penis tried to beat a hasty retreat into my abdomen when it spotted that needle—I had the cock-length in that moment of a child hermaphrodite—but the doctor, a skilled physician, found his mark and that needle hurt profoundly. I have to say that watching it sink in didn't help matters.

Well, it was all deeply traumatic and I couldn't say the word "wart" after visiting the doctor. I could only refer to the thing as a "W"—the whole word was too reprehensible to me—and I was forever thinking that my W was coming back. I should repeat that this was in the year 1984, long before the current president was in office.

So because of my incessant worrying about my W having a second term, I often combined a visit to my parents with a visit to the dermatologist, but he never found anything. I would be relieved, but also disappointed: I had come to think of my W as physical proof of all the self-loathing things I thought about myself. What a waste of time (my whole life) if they weren't true, and I wanted the truth to come out. On my penis. In the form of a wart. And then I wanted the wart removed. Immediately. I wanted to be purified, forgiven. It was a painful purification, but then I would be good. I would be clean.

You see, my mental-emotional cycle has always been that of the phoenix: On a subconscious level, though I'm conscious of it as I write this, I feel the need to continually destroy myself and then rebuild myself. Destroy, rebuild. Destroy, rebuild. Hence my desire back then for the W to reappear: I would get to hate myself for having it, but then I'd get to have it removed. Hate, remove = destroy, rebuild. But the W wasn't complying: It wouldn't come back. How could I play the phoenix without a W?

But in 1989, after waiting for half a decade for it to come back, this obsession with my W finally almost did bring about my desired destruction. The near-fatal blow happened in Europe. In January of that year, I had put together a little money and decided to live in Paris for a few months.

In early February, I left Paris to visit an old romantic interest in the German city of Kiel. I arrived in that somber, gray North Sea metropolis in the morning, after a nineteen-hour train ride, and my old girlfriend, whom I hadn't seen since 1983, met me on the platform and said to me, "You're fifteen minutes late."

I had forgotten how German she was. I was fifteen minutes late after a nineteen-hour journey! Did she think I was responsible for the train's tardiness? I didn't know what to say, so I just handed her the flowers I had picked up at the previous station. She took them, kissed me on the cheek, and then led me to her car.

Her name was Marisol and she was a well-put-together blonde with green eyes. I had high hopes that we would rekindle our old love affair, but waiting in her car was her fiancé of three weeks. I had come all the way to Kiel because of a miscommunication: She wanted to see me, I wanted to resume our old love-affair. She wanted to surprise me with the wonderful news of her engagement, I wanted to get back on the train.

Her fiancé, Gunther, was a giant of a young man, at least six-five, whose head, at the top, had dents on the right and left sides. This may have been from a forceps birth or he simply had a large and pronounced skull, which is often the case with abnormally tall Northern European men. His skin was that cheese-textured German pale, and as we shook hands he regarded me with distrust and dislike; there may have also been a healthy dose of disrespect. What an awkward situation for us two males, but there was no polite way for me to flee—Marisol would have been terribly offended if I bolted—and since I'm usually not capable of profound acts of rudeness, I had to go along as if everything was all right. So I sat in the back of Gunther's tiny Volkswagen, his head touched the ceiling as he drove, and Marisol, in the front seat, twisted about and smiled at me, updating me on her life and her engagement.

Marisol and Gunther were law students, and they had met, Marisol informed me, in school the year before, and the wedding was to be in the summer, and I would surely be invited. We had hardly been in touch for six years—I had come to Kiel for a simple romantic rekindling—and now I was being invited to her wedding.

That afternoon she and Gunther had exams and so they dropped me off at Marisol's apartment. She said, "I'll be back tonight. We'll have a party for finishing our tests."

She left me with a key and I went to a small bakery-cum-cafe and ate pastries and drank coffee. Coffee in Europe always raises the spirits and so I decided that I would try to make the best of this trip to Kiel. I then opened the book I had brought with me: *The Once and Future King*. I had purchased it in Paris from a used-book dealer. I hadn't read it since high school, but I looked forward to revisiting this comic telling of the Arthurian legend. The second sentence of the book read as follows: "The governess was always getting muddled with her astrolabe, and when she got specially muddled she would take it out of the Wart by rapping his knuckles."

Wart. This stopped me. I had forgotten that King Arthur was called Wart as a boy. The fourth sentence read: "The Wart was called the Wart because it more or less rhymed with Art, which was short for his real name."

I shuddered a little seeing the word "Wart" so often, and then I needed to use the toilet because of the strong coffee. Reading about King Arthur made me think that I had better check myself out, and so, as I urinated, I was sure that I saw the W. I finished peeing and looked at my penis closely. There *was* a W!

I was now trapped in Kiel, Germany. Who knew what kind of dermatologists they had. I ran back to Marisol's apartment and broke into her beer supply in the refrigerator. I'm only supposed to drink temperance beverages—I can't handle liquor—but I couldn't bear the idea of having the W so far from home. I wanted it taken care of right away. I needed immediate atonement. Short of that, oblivion through intoxication seemed to be my only recourse.

Marisol and Gunther came back from their exams in good spirits. They had started drinking at school—champagne—and so they didn't mind my inebriated state. I was pretending to be jolly with the happy couple, but I was dying inside. Gunther, a bit tipsy, was a little kinder to me now. He was firmly established as the alpha male in our little threesome, and my ancient fornicating with his wife-to-be was now a distant, unimportant episode of her youth.

We went out for dinner—I repaired to the bathroom several times and studied my W—and we drank more, and then they took me to a party at a fraternity house for law students. Marisol and Gunther weren't members, but anyone could attend the party. We positioned ourselves at a long oak bar and I was having many tall glasses of nuclear-powered German beer. I was drunk as hell and thinking a lot about my

W. The room was crowded and smoky. There were blonde women and cheese-textured pale men. I noted that many of the young men had scars on their cheeks. This distracted me momentarily from my W thoughts, and I queried Marisol about all the scar tissue on the males. She explained to me that the scars were the result of an initiation ritual—the fraternity members would stand on boxes and strike each other with sabres. The idea was not to move. The scar was a sign of bravery.

Marisol and Gunther went off to mingle with friends. I drank more. I was maudlin and pathetic. I had used many poor excuses to drink, but a W on my penis was one of the most ridiculous.

I propped myself against the bar. What was I doing in Germany? My parents wouldn't ride in Volkswagens when I was growing up. I drunkenly thought that maybe the return of the W was my punishment for being in the land where many of my relatives had been persecuted and killed. I then felt the need to redeem myself for my betrayal of my people, and I got it in my drunken head that I should challenge one of the scarred law students to a duel. So I said to the fellow next to me, "I'm a Jew, you know. And I've trained as a swordsman and I have come back for revenge. I'm the result of a Jewish experiment in the 1940s to create blond Jews to infiltrate the Nazi party, but the war ended before we could put this into action. But here I am now and I'm going to kick your ass."

At the time, I had a full head of blond hair and was often mistaken for being Swedish. Where I came up with this Jewish science-experiment notion, I have no idea. I was completely nuts from the booze and the W paranoia, and the

German fellow I had verbally assaulted understood everything I said—almost all Germans speak English beautifully—but before I could tell this scarred law student to get the sabres, he pushed me in the chest. I then pushed him back, the expected primitive response. He then punched me in my right pectoral muscle—somehow missing my chin. I then took a swing at him and my fist glanced off his shoulder. He responded by punching me in the neck and I began to choke. Gunther, out of nowhere, came to my rescue. He shoved my fight partner hard to the bar. It was incredibly decent of him. My opponent backed off. Gunther, as I mentioned, was an imposing figure.

Gunther then dragged me out of the fraternity house and Marisol followed. I stopped choking and vomited in the street. They took me home. I vomited in the bathroom. When I was done in there, they put me on the couch with a garbage can next to me and then they said good night and went into Marisol's bedroom. I was happy for Gunther, my protector, my friend. He had gone from not liking me at the train station to being downright affectionate and I felt the same way about him. In the car back to the apartment, he had said, "I never met an American like you."

After they left me on the couch, I tried to take my sweater off, but was too drunk to do it. At one point, it got stuck on my head and I nearly affixiated. I drunkenly prayed to Jack Kerouac, F. Scott Fitzgerald, and Ernest Hemingway to help me get the sweater off my head and for them to see me through the night. I was scared that I might die from being stuck in my sweater or by choking to death on my own vomit, like Jimi Hendrix. At the time, F. Scott, Hemingway, and Jack K. were

my three favorite writers, and I smartly reasoned that they all
had experience with booze-related near-death experiences and
that they would take pity on me.

In the morning, I was sick and hungover. I made it worse
by going to the bathroom and looking at King Arthur on my
penis. And then I looked in the mirror. I had a large purple
bruise on my Adam's apple. It hurt to swallow. I could have
been killed in that fight. All because of my W.

Marisol and Gunther were still asleep. I wrote them a
note, apologizing profusely for my behavior, and asked both
of them to forget that they ever knew me.

I walked to the station. I saw that there was a train for
Berlin in an hour. I decided to go there in honor of Christopher Isherwood, another writer I admired, and I came up
with the plan that in Berlin I would find a prostitute, wear
a condom so as not to give her the W, and then kill myself.
I may have still been drunk from the night before.

While I waited for the train, Marisol and Gunther came
and found me. Marisol was very angry with me for sneaking off. "How dare you leave like that," she said, and she was
right. But Gunther found it all very exciting, and he pleaded
with me not to go. His affection for me was growing by leaps
and bounds. "You're a real crazy writer," he said. "I want to
know you, talk to you about life." He was associating alcoholic, psychopathic behavior with the practice of the literary arts, and he was not wrong to do so—though there was
also an implication that the practice of said arts gave me
access to wisdom about "life," which, clearly, was patently
false. He was kind to suggest that I had such access, but I
was not swayed by his supplication. I told him and Marisol

that I was having a mental breakdown and couldn't burden them further. Ultimately, they relented and allowed me to board the train.

I later received a letter from Marisol in Paris in which she expressed great concern about my health and well-being and told me that she and Gunther eagerly awaited word from me—reassurances that I had recovered from my breakdown and that I was all right. I was so embarrassed, though, by my time in Kiel that I never wrote to her. It's a real black mark in my dealings with the world, and I guess in this day and age of the Internet I could find her and write her a long-overdue apology, but perhaps some people from the past are better left alone. I do hope that she and Gunther are indeed happily married—an invitation to the wedding, understandably, never came—and that they share a thriving law practice and have several children.

Anyway, I did go to Berlin. I got on that train and leaned out the window and waved good-bye to Marisol and Gunther. I felt like a tragic-romantic figure in a World War II movie, and as I waved, I thought once more of my plan: I'm going to get a prostitute and then I'm going to kill myself. Thinking this while waving at them made me feel doubly tragic—if they only knew!

I drank on the train, arrived in Berlin in the early afternoon, got a hotel room, and then went out and kept on drinking. It's a bit of a blur, but I managed to get arrested at Checkpoint Charlie—the Berlin Wall was still in place at the time. Some West German fellow in a bar had convinced me to buy East German money from him. I then tried to go to East Berlin—I thought I should engage in some tourism before committing suicide—and I had that East German money on me and it was discovered by the border guards when they asked me if I had any such money. I naively said that I did—I didn't know it was against the law—and I was then kept in a room for two hours and was yelled at for being drunk and having illegal currency, which they confiscated and didn't return. I also had to pay the equivalent of a $25 fine. Luckily, I was so drunk that I didn't much mind this confrontation with the authorities. Normally, I would have been petrified and would have confessed to crimes I hadn't even committed, but the booze saw me through the whole thing, though, of course, I wouldn't have been detained if I wasn't drunk in the first place.

They released me into East Berlin and I kept drinking over there and I found it to be much more beautiful than West Berlin. The West got the money and the East got the architecture.

I returned to the West in the late evening, and my will to kill myself was dissipating somewhat, but I felt I should go through with it, that I should show character and not deviate from my plan. But before I found a prostitute and then killed myself, I stumbled into a peep show. It was a rather high-tech German sort of place and on a wall were glossy photos of pretty girls. I managed to deduce that I could pick one of the girls in the photos and actually talk to her in a private booth. I chose a fine representative of the Teutonic ideal—blonde with ample breasts—and we met in the booth, which had an odd setup. The young woman was on an elevated stage about a foot high and there was a clear plastic shield between us, which came up to her breasts. The effect of the stage was that her boobs were at my eye level and the rest of her, because of the plastic, was off-limits.

She asked me if I was American, and I whispered shyly that I was, and then she told me in English that I could masturbate in front of her for a certain price and that I could touch her breasts and masturbate at the same time for another price. Being shy, I chose to just touch her breasts, which cost the same as touching and masturbating, but I didn't care. So I began to touch her breasts, and they felt wonderful—heavy but soft—and she was awfully beautiful. Light from behind her gave her an angelic glow, illuminating the delicate hairs between her slightly parted legs. I, on the other hand, stood in a dark shadow, while gently caressing her.

Then she put her hand behind my head and guided me to her breasts. She fed me one of her lovely nipples and encouraged me sweetly, with her stroking of my hair, to nurse as much as I liked. "You seem sad," she said. Her English was flawless, and so was her psychological insight. I nursed for about five minutes—an eternity in the world of peep shows—and all thoughts of self-destruction completely evaporated. The power of the life-giving female breast!

I don't know why that woman was so kind and generous to me, but I've often been lucky this way in life, finding people in the most unusual places and circumstances to take care of me.

When my time was up, I thanked her, she smiled warmly at me, and then I returned to my hotel. I lay in bed and had alcoholic hallucinations—small bodies were moving in the wallpaper—but I didn't kill myself. I was twenty-five years old and I was still alive. The next afternoon, I went back to the peep show to see her again, but she wasn't there—her picture wasn't on the wall. I was very disappointed but since I was there I chose another girl; I'm nothing if not weak. I was told the same prices and options as the day before but I asked this new girl if I could kiss her breasts. "Oh, no," she said, "that's not allowed." This shocked me and made what had happened the night before seem even more incredible.

I thought of staying in Berlin until that first woman came back to the peep show, even if I had to wait days, but then I decided against it. I didn't want to mar what had been an amazing exchange.

That evening, I took a train back to Paris and then cut short my time there so that I could return to the States and go to my dermatologist. When I saw him, he thoroughly inspected my penis, and there was no W. What I'd thought was a W was a hair follicle without a hair. "Are you sure?" I asked the doctor.

"I'm sure," he said, and against my better judgment, I believed him.

2004

JERSEY SHORE

I'm sitting on a train in Hoboken, waiting to go home to visit my parents. A few minutes ago, I stepped outside the station and I heard seagulls. I love the sound of seagulls. I imagine a lot of people love that sound, though I don't recall anyone ever telling me about it. But I know that it's not a unique love. It's like my love of dogs. Everyone loves dogs. I'm not very original in the things I love. But I don't really care. I still love dogs with all my heart.

I must love the sound of seagulls because of my childhood. Every summer for about ten years—kind of the golden years of my childhood—we went to the Jersey Shore. The two-and-a-half-hour ride in the car always seemed to be horribly endless to my sister and me. But we felt such joy, such mad happiness when we would finally pull into the parking lot of the Sea Shell Motel in Beach Haven and we would be released at last from the car. We would run right to the beach. As I ran, I probably heard seagulls.

Then we'd come back and help our parents carry the bags in, and the lobby of the Sea Shell always smelled like chlorine from a small fountain they had, and just as I love the sound of seagulls, I also have loved the smell of chlorine ever since. It means the same thing as seagulls to me—happiness.

We'd spend a week at the Sea Shell. It was the highlight of my whole year, but, unfortunately, this was the early 1970s and sunblock hadn't been invented yet. So every summer I would get a terrible sunburn. Just a few days ago I had sizable pieces of precancerous flesh removed from my back. I'm loaded with uncomfortable stitches which don't feel good at all against this train seat. When I get home, my father will clean my wounds and put on fresh bandages. I have to get someone to do this for me twice a day, which isn't easy when you live alone. I wish I could reach the stitches and do it myself, but I can't.

My father will clean me up because he loves me. I'm not sure why he loves me—I'm never sure why anyone loves me; is it something we can know?—but my father does. So he'll clean my wounds from those long-ago summers, summers that I loved, summers that I still love in my mind.

2005

Your-forties-are-actually-your-thirties (yor-for'tees-ar-ack'choo'al'lee-yor-thur'tees), n. A person's age. Originally, a person's forties were a person's forties. But then, in 2013, an error was discovered in the Modern Calendar. Thus, like a gigantic daylight savings time, all people who were in their forties were allowed to return to their thirties. And people who were in their fifties were actually in their forties, and people who were in their sixties were actually in their fifties, and so on. This made the whole world quite happy, as everyone had always wished to be at least a decade younger. And since everything was so confused and messed up, though in a good way, all governments dropped mandatory retirement. You could now retire if and when you wanted, and some people did and some people didn't, which is emblematic of most things in life. People in their thirties were, due to some bizarre mathematical anomaly, still in their thirties, but they didn't mind this, as the thirties are a pretty good age—you're just starting to panic about growing old, but not really. The same went for twenty-somethings, teenagers, and small children—they all stayed at their right age, but they didn't complain, since they all still believed that they would live forever anyway, which is a wonderful state of mind, though it does account for a certain laxness when it comes to wearing seat belts in automobiles.

S/HE SAID, HE SAID

I met Jonathan Ames in a small cafe in his Boerum Hill, Brooklyn, neighborhood to discuss *Sexual Metamorphosis: An Anthology of Transsexual Memoirs,* which Ames edited and for which he wrote the introduction. He arrived ten minutes late, even though he lives only a block from the cafe. "I'm sorry," he said, "I'm congenitally ten minutes late for everything. I really apologize." I told him it was not a problem, that I have the same issue. But what turned out to be a problem was our interview. We began in person in the cafe, but then things took a bad turn and so we had to complete the interview over e-mail. The two parts of our "conversation" will be simply marked Part I and Part II.

Part I

JA: Are you a tranny-chaser?
JA: What's a "tranny-chaser"?

JA: Come on. Don't be coy.

JA: Did you say "goy"?

JA: No, "coy."

JA: Oh, I thought that maybe you said "Don't be goy" because I wasn't fessing up to something. You know, like I was showing WASPish restraint or something.

JA: No, I said "coy," because you've written about transsexuals quite a lot. Like in your novel *The Extra Man*.

JA: Yeah, but that's a novel. Novels are fiction. Fiction means you make stuff up.

JA: Well, you've also written about transsexuals in your nonfiction essays.

JA: (*silent*)

JA: And now you've edited this book all about transsexuals, so just answer the question: Are you a tranny-chaser or not?

JA: Is that tape recorder working?

JA: The red light is on—that means it's working.

JA: Check it. Just to make sure. Sometimes I've been interviewed and the thing doesn't work and we have to start all over and it's kind of, you know, frustrating.

JA: (*I check the tape recorder. It's working.*) Listen, I'm sorry if I put you on the spot with that first question. I can start with something else.

JA: It's all right. It's a legitimate question.

JA: So you do know what "tranny-chaser" means?

JA: Yes, I know what it means! Do you know what it means?

JA: It means someone who chases trannies. Who likes to have sex with trannies.

JA: (*Ames stands up.*) You know, I'm not usually good at protecting myself and having boundaries because of some weird erotic childhood abuse I suffered and enjoyed. So I let people do whatever they want with me. But I'm working on this. So fuck you and have a nice life. (*Ames walks out. Thirty seconds later, he walks back in.*) I'm really sorry. I almost never curse. That was bad. Let's do this over e-mail. Okay? When I write I can be sort of honest. In person, it's too personal. You know?

JA: No problem. I'll e-mail you.

JA: You know my e-mail?

JA: Yeah.

Part II

JonathanAmes2@aol.com: I didn't get a chance to say it the other day, but I'm sorry about what happened in the cafe, and I hope we can make this work in e-mail. So, can you tell me how & why you came to put this book together?

JonathanAmes2@aol.com: Before I answer that, let me address what happened in the cafe. The reason why I got upset about the tranny-chaser question is this: Tranny-chasing is usually a reference to someone who likes pre-op transsexual prostitutes. But most pre-op transsexual prostitutes do not want sex-change surgery, and this book is about people who have undergone sex-change surgery. So I felt like you were making this about me and not about the book, since the book has nothing to do with tranny-chasing.

But looking over what I just wrote, I realize that pre-op transsexual prostitutes shouldn't be called "pre-ops" anymore. There's some kind of cultural shift going on. When I first started hanging out with tranny prostitutes in 1992 (to do research for *The Extra Man*), most of the trannies spoke of someday getting the surgery. But nowadays almost none of the girls talk about it. "I like my cock," they say, or "I like myself the way I am, why should I change?" Stuff like that. They've become more pro-cock or something. It's weird. Also, they refer to themselves as transies, not trannies. So I think the phrase "tranny-chaser" is probably outdated. It probably should be "transy-chaser."

JonathanAmes2@aol.com: So are you a transy-chaser?

JonathanAmes2@aol.com: No, I'm not a transy-chaser! Or a tranny-chaser. In my youth, back in the early '90s, more than twelve years ago, I might have been classified as such. But not now.

JonathanAmes2@aol.com: But you wrote "nowadays almost none of the girls . . ." This would seem to imply that you're still in the scene.

JonathanAmes2@aol.com: Is this an interview or a cross-examination? I'm not in the scene anymore! Occasionally, though, out of habit and nostalgia, I dip back in and visit a tranny club. My interest, the titillation I receive, is from being in the presence of something that is "other." And this may run parallel to the girls being more pro-cock. Perhaps they feel less of a need to completely transform, that they are satisfied with being other. They're not female, they're not male, they're other. And a sexual other in the 21st century has somehow become more acceptable, even though the U.S. is now a theocracy.

JonathanAmes2@aol.com: I like what you wrote in your last e-mail, but can you briefly tell me how & why you put this book together?

JonathanAmes2@aol.com: Okay. In 2001, I was sent the memoir of a transsexual—*The Woman I Was Not Born to Be* by Aleshia Brevard—to blurb. I read the book and realized that Aleshia had picked me up in 1990 in a bar in Pennsylvania. It was a December-May thing, and I was May. She was in her early fifties and I was 26. We had a few kisses that night and I never saw her again. At the time, in 1990, I thought she was a biological woman. Then I got her memoir eleven years later, which was, obviously, an incredible coincidence. It was like something out of a Paul Auster novel, but perverted. I blurbed the book, and Aleshia and I had a very nice reunion in San Francisco in 2002.

Anyway, after reading Aleshia's memoir in 2001, I noticed a rash of books that seemed to be about gender: *Suits Me: The Double Life of Billy Tipton,* by Diane Middlebrook, which is about Tipton, a woman who passed as a man for years, fooling the jazz world and, supposedly, his/her own wife; *As Nature Made Him,* by John Colapinto, which is about the boy who lost his penis in a botched circumcision and was raised as a girl; and *Crossing,* by Deirdre McCloskey, which is the memoir of a University of Illinois economics professor who underwent sex-change surgery.

Also, around this time, Jonathan Lethem gave me a copy of *The Vintage Book of Amnesia,* which he edited, and I thought: I want to put together an anthology, it looks like easy money. So I asked Lethem how much he was paid for the book and he gave me a rather high number, which turned out to be all wrong. But I didn't discover this until much later. Thus, spurred by visions of money, combined with the confluence of all these gender books, I got the idea in my head for an anthology whose unifying theme would be the changing of one's sex. I was going to include transsexual memoirs, the Middlebrook and Colapinto books, some stuff on hermaphrodites and transvestites, and works of fiction which featured transsexuals. Gore Vidal, Jerzy Kosinski, John Irving, and David Ebershoff all had novels which qualified on this front, and I figured I could self-promote and include a passage from *The Extra Man*.

I was teaching then at Indiana University, so I used the Kinsey Library and xeroxed about a thousand pages of material and sent it off to Vintage. They made an offer that was one third of what Lethem had told me he got. I checked with him and he realized he had made a mistake.

I was disappointed but I took their offer, and the editor and I decided I should whittle the book down just to the memoirs of transsexuals. Then it was such a pain in the ass to get permissions—I had naively thought Vintage would do this for me—that I didn't do anything with the book for years. I kept waiting to make some money from Hollywood so that I could pay Vintage back the first part of my advance. Then some money from Hollywood did come in and instead of giving up on the anthology, which I had been privately referring to as the "tranthology," I hired someone and he did everything and now the book is out! So the book is about sex and I did it for money. A classic tale!

JonathanAmes2@aol.com: I think I've got enough now for the article. Thank you!

JonathanAmes2@aol.com: You're welcome! Sorry, again, about the cafe!

JonathanAmes2@aol.com: I forgive you!

2005

MIDLIFE ASSESSMENT: CATALOGING MY RUINATION

I'm forty-one years old and I'm absolutely falling apart. I'll start from the top and work my way down, cataloging, as it were, my disintegration.

I am bald, except for the sides of my head. All the stuff at the top has just about melted away. There are a few resilient, aberrant strands, so I buzz my hair down with clippers so that I don't look like I have mange.

My eyes, from staring at a computer all day, are often blurry and in pain. I bought reading glasses a few years ago, but they are so smudged that I think they are making my eyes worse. I shouldn't stare at the computer so much, but I'm addicted to Internet backgammon and I'm a writer, which means I spend my days writing e-mails. The collective word count of all my e-mails would surely equal Tolstoy's *War and Peace*.

Inside my head, behind my eyes and beneath my bald dome, is a lingering, mild depression, which causes me to procrastinate and not do simple tasks like cleaning my reading glasses or to begin important tasks like writing my version of *War and Peace*. Generally speaking, my depression manifests itself as this feeling of subtle displacement from my life. I'm reminded of this line from the movie *The Red Shoes:* "Life rushes by, time rushes by, but the red shoes go on dancing forever." All of that applies to me, except for the red shoes part. Everything seems to be rushing by, and I'm floating above it all, reaching my hand out to life, but not quite grasping it, like waving your hand for a taxi that is clearly occupied.

My nose gives me a lot of trouble. When I was five years old, I was attacked by a disturbed youth, and he broke my small, just-forming beak. This did something to a vein inside my nose and ever since I've had hundreds, if not thousands, of nosebleeds. This past winter, my nosebleeds were the worst they've ever been. The heating in my apartment baked the interior of my nostrils, and I had two or three nosebleeds a day. I thought of going to a blood bank and hooking up my nose to some kind of contraption and earning some extra cash. Naturally, I exacerbate the situation with the occasional unconscious exploration of my nostrils with a digit (i.e., finger), while nervously playing Internet backgammon. There's nothing more humiliating than bleeding on your laptop from nose-picking while wasting time playing Internet backgammon.

Of all my body parts, my mouth is in pretty good shape. Not having dental insurance, I haven't been to a dentist in years, but I bought a tooth scraper in a drugstore and take great pleasure in removing my own plaque and tartar, which sounds like the name of a law firm. Just this morning I spent at least fifteen minutes on my plaque, and I'm always amazed how quickly it comes back. It's sort of like my massive credit card bills. Every month I pay them and I experience this naive sense of satisfaction that this will be the last time I ever have to do that again. But there they are the next month. Plaque and debt are clearly spiritual brothers. One area of concern in my mouth is my front right tooth. It is half fake and completely yellow but rapidly moving toward brown. I fell in a bathtub when I was six and chipped my tooth, and the cap hasn't been replaced in twenty-one years. But this tooth gives me character; it is kind of like a mood ring, growing darker each year as I grow increasingly strange.

My neck is no good. I can't turn my head when I parallel park. I'm like the Seabiscuit jockey, who didn't let people know he was half blind. I don't let people know that I can't actually turn my head.

My right shoulder was pulverized by my enormous nineteen-year-old son. He still likes to have "tickle-time," though now it's called "Let's wrestle," which means that he attacks me without warning and injures me terribly. I'm kind of like Inspector Clouseau and he's Kato, except in this instance Kato weighs two hundred pounds, is six foot one, and combines his Oedipal complex with a passion for weight lifting. One of my son's attacks—he sprang from behind a door and threw me to the ground, while giggling—is the cause of my shoulder problem. I've been unable to fully extend my right arm over my head ever since. Oddly enough, it's also very painful for me to reach across my body and retrieve my wallet from a sport-coat pocket. So an act that previously had been symbolically painful (see above reference to massive credit-card debt) is now literally hurtful.

Recently, I got health insurance for the first time in years, and so I decided to see a doctor about my shoulder. The fellow spent about one minute with me and pronounced that I have either tendonitis or a torn rotator cuff. It's unclear. I was sent for physical therapy, which I greatly enjoyed. It was kind of like a gym for hypochondriacs. I told the physical therapist about the chair I sat in to do my e-mail writing—an old wooden chair I found on the street twelve years ago—and he said it was damaging my neck *and* my shoulder. So I purchased an inexpensive office chair. I sat in it for a day, and my lower back went numb. The physical therapist said this was because I hadn't sat properly in a chair for years. Anyway, my shoulder still doesn't work, and my lower back is still numb, but I like my chair because it has wheels.

In the last six months, I have had three precancerous moles removed from my right shoulder, middle back, and abdomen. I've received over a dozen stitches. The hole in my abdomen, like something out of a Kafka story, has not healed, and I'm procrastinating about going back to the doctor. Surely it's not normal to have a hole in one's abdomen going on four months now.

Not long ago, after playing a marathon game of Wiffle ball with my son, a strange lump formed in the palm of my right hand. I noticed the lump the next day when I ran my hand over my bald head and in some weird sensory mistake thought that the lump—a brain tumor?!?—was on the skull. I looked in the mirror at my head, didn't see any tumor, and then looked at my hand and saw a lump the size of a marble. Something about the way I grabbed the plastic Wiffle-ball bat must have inflamed the sensitive tendons in my hand. It's a painful lump, and it announces itself when I grasp the steering wheel while parallel parking. The benefit, though, of this palm-lump pain is that it distracts me temporarily from my neck pain.

My stomach is actually good these days. In 2001, I had irritable bowel syndrome brought on by heartbreak and was seriously thinking of getting fitted for a diaper. I was a walking scatological time bomb. But my heart healed and my intestines followed suit. My libido is down by about 40 percent, but this is probably a blessing, though my weakened sex drive may be linked to the existential displacement described above.

The lower third of my body, I have to say, is also in excellent shape, except that my right ankle is frozen and probably in the early stages of arthritis, but debilitation-wise it's nothing to write home about. Not yet anyway.

Well, I've run out of body parts, and I'm rather relieved. If I had any more depressing limbs or organs to discuss, I might not have been able to finish writing this catalog of my ruination. I have noted that my disintegration, like some kind of spreading tree rot, has only reached my ribs, where the Kafkaesque hole is. I don't think there's anything I can do to stop this rot from spreading further, but at least I can watch its progress, as I might watch the lengthening of a shadow at the end of the day as light fades and darkness predominates.

2005

THE ONION ASKS ME: WHAT IS FUNNY?

My ass was itchy for fifteen years. I never knew why but I thought maybe it was coffee. So sometimes I would quit coffee for a day, but then I'd break down and drink it the next day. Thus, there was no way to know if coffee was causing the ass-itch, but I definitely suspected it for fifteen years, and I have to say that the pleasure I took in coffee was greatly diminished.

Then I wrote an article for a newspaper about how my ass had been itchy my whole adulthood and a lot of people wrote to me—mostly fellow sufferers. One guy wrote that he hadn't left his house for years because he didn't want to scratch himself in public. Who knows how many agoraphobes are actually people with ass problems.

The best letter came from a kindly scientist who told me that I probably had athlete's foot in my ass. He was a physicist and had cured himself of a twenty-three-year ass-itch with athlete's foot powder. So I got some foot powder and put it in my ass and it worked! I couldn't believe it! I enjoyed my coffee for the first time in years. I said to my girlfriend, "I have athlete's foot in my ass."

She said, "Which athlete?"

I then imagined an athlete's cleat sticking out of my butt and I really laughed, which I think is a fitting end to this tale, this anecdote, which has been my way of answering that age-old question: What is funny?

2005

Self-loathing Self-portrait

ACKNOWLEDGMENTS

I would like to thank and acknowledge Tom Beller, Dara Hyde, Rosalie Siegel, John Strausbaugh, and all the editors who have kindly published my work.